DATE DUE

GAMBLING

Gambling

EXAMINING POP CULTURE

JAMES HALEY, Book Editor

Daniel Leone, President
Bonnie Szumski, Publisher
Scott Barbour, Managing Editor

GREENHAVEN
PRESS®

THOMSON
━━━━━✦━━━━━ ™
GALE

San Diego • Detroit • New York • San Francisco • Cleveland
New Haven, Conn. • Waterville, Maine • London • Munich

For more information, contact
Greenhaven Press
27500 Drake Rd.
Farmington Hills, MI 48331-3535
Or you can visit our Internet site at http://www.gale.com

Cover credit: © Photofest

LIBRARY OF CONGRESS CATALOGING-IN-PUBLICATION DATA

Gambling / James Haley, book editor.
    p. cm.—(Examining pop culture)
Includes bibliographical references and index.
ISBN 0-7377-1638-X (pbk. : alk. paper) — ISBN 0-7377-1637-1 (lib. : alk. paper)
    1. Gambling—United States. 2. Gambling—Social aspects—United States.
3. Popular culture—United States. I. Haley, James, 1968– . II. Series: Examining pop culture.
HV6715.G285   2004
306.4'82'0973—dc21
                                                                    2003054035

Printed in the United States of America

CONTENTS

resorts. The relentless strip redefined leisure for Americans as an exciting consumer activity that challenged the conformity of mainstream life.

Chapter 3: Games People Play

barges have become big business, and citizens have grown to accept gambling as a valuable source of jobs and taxable revenue.

FOREWORD

POPULAR CULTURE IS THE COMMON SET OF ARTS, entertainments, customs, beliefs, and values shared by large segments of society. Russel B. Nye, one of the founders of the study of popular culture, wrote that "not until the appearance of mass society in the eighteenth century could popular culture, as one now uses the term, be said to exist." According to Nye, the Industrial Revolution and the rise of democracy in the eighteenth and nineteenth centuries led to increased urbanization and the emergence of a powerful middle class. In nineteenth-century Europe and North America, these trends created audiences for the popular arts that were larger, more concentrated, and more well off than at any point in history. As a result, more people shared a common culture than ever before.

The technological advancements of the twentieth century vastly accelerated the spread of popular culture. With each new advance in mass communication—motion pictures, radio, television, and the Internet—popular culture has become an increasingly pervasive aspect of everyday life.

Popular entertainment—in the form of movies, television, theater, music recordings and concerts, books, magazines, sporting events, video games, restaurants, casinos, theme parks, and other attractions—is one very recognizable aspect of popular culture. In his 1999 book *The Entertainment Economy: How Mega-Media Forces Are Transforming Our Lives*, Michael J. Wolf argues that entertainment is becoming the dominant feature of American society: "In choosing where we buy French fries, how we relate to political candidates, what airline we want to fly, what pajamas we choose for our kids, and which mall we want to buy them in, entertainment is increasingly influencing every one of those choices. . . . Multiply that by the billions of choices that, collectively, all of us make each day and you have a portrait of a society in which entertainment is one of its leading institutions."

It is partly this pervasive quality of popular culture that makes it worthy of study. James Combs, the author of *Polpop: Politics and Popular Culture in America*, explains that examining popular culture is important because it can shape people's attitudes and beliefs:

> Popular culture is so much a part of our lives that we cannot deny its developmental powers. . . . Like formal education or family rearing, popular culture is part of our "learning environment.". . . Though our pop culture education is informal—we usually do not attend to pop culture for its "educational" value—it nevertheless provides us with information and images upon which we develop our opinions and attitudes. We would not be what we are, nor would our society be quite the same, without the impact of popular culture.

Examining popular culture is also important because popular movies, music, fads, and the like often reflect popular opinions and attitudes. Christopher D. Geist and Jack Nachbar explain in *The Popular Culture Reader*, "the popular arts provide a gauge by which we can learn what Americans are thinking, their fears, fantasies, dreams, and dominant mythologies. The popular arts reflect the values of the multitude."

This two-way relationship between popular culture and society is evident in many modern discussions of popular culture. Does the glorification of guns by many rap artists, for example, merely reflect the realities of inner-city life, or does it also contribute to the problem of gun violence? Such questions also arise in discussions of the popular culture of the past. Did the Vietnam protest music of the late 1960s and early 1970s, for instance, simply reflect popular antiwar sentiments, or did it help turn public opinion against the war? Examining such questions is an important part of understanding history.

Greenhaven Press's *Examining Pop Culture* series provides students with the resources to begin exploring these questions. Each volume in the series focuses on a particular aspect of popular culture, with topics as varied as popular culture itself. Books in the series may focus on a particular genre, such as *Rap and Hip Hop*, while others may cover a specific medium, such as *Computers and the Internet*. Volumes such as *Body Piercing and Tattoos* have their focus on recent trends in popular culture, while titles like *Americans' Views About War* have a broader historical scope.

In each volume, an introductory essay provides a general

overview of the topic. The selections that follow offer a survey of critical thought about the subject. The readings in *Americans' Views About War*, for example, are arranged chronologically: Essays explore how popular films, songs, television programs, and even comic books both reflected and shaped public opinion about American wars from World War I through Vietnam. The essays in *Violence in Film and Television*, on the other hand, take a more varied approach: Some provide historical background, while others examine specific genres of violent film, such as horror, and still others discuss the current controversy surrounding the issue.

Each book in the series contains a comprehensive index to help readers quickly locate material of interest. Perhaps most importantly, each volume has an annotated bibliography to aid interested students in conducting further research on the topic. In today's culture, what is "popular" changes rapidly from year to year and even month to month. Those who study popular culture must constantly struggle to keep up. The volumes in Greenhaven's *Examining Pop Culture* series are intended to introduce readers to the major themes and issues associated with each topic, so they can begin examining for themselves what impact popular culture has on their own lives.

SINCE THE LATE 1970S THE UNITED STATES HAS experienced a boom in legalized gambling. Once confined to Nevada and a handful of other states, some form of legalized gambling—lotteries, casinos, card rooms, horse racing, or video poker—can now be found in every state in the union, with the exception of Hawaii and Utah. On first inspection, the current boom may appear as something of an anomaly in a nation settled by Puritans, who shunned the temptations of luck and instant gratification in favor of hard work and bootstrap ascendancy up the economic ladder. The much-vaunted Protestant work ethic is certainly an ingrained feature of American life, but gambling has deep roots in the United States and has enjoyed persistent popularity despite periods of prohibition brought about by social reformers, politicians, and religious crusaders. Gambling's popularity betrays countervailing cultural values of risk, competition, and the desire for quick riches against which monkish prudence never stood much of a chance. After all, the country was founded on speculation and the promise of a better life; it was settled by people who chanced it all to start their lives over in a land that beckoned with the religious freedom and economic opportunity absent in their homelands. From the original thirteen colonies to the Pacific coast, gambling emerged as an activity that went hand in hand with the nation's speculative character and frontier spirit. Although some critics do not like what the popularity of gambling says about Americans—namely, that they are selfish, greedy, disdainful of work, and addicted to instant gratification—gambling may be an irrepressible outgrowth of cultural values that are deeply ingrained in the national psyche.

The Rise of Gambling in the Expanding Territories

Gambling activity appeared early on in American history as an outward expression of the individualism and competition for wealth that characterized the nascent society of the New World. Once arrived in the colonies, settlers discovered that risk taking became a way of life. With its minerals, timber, and seemingly endless farmland, the frontier held the possibility of untold riches yet required a willingness to venture forth into the unknown. Gambling's pervasive hold on the burgeoning popular culture would become most evident following the Louisiana Purchase in 1803, which opened the vast western frontier to American settlement. President Thomas Jefferson bought the Louisiana territory from French ruler Napoléon Bonaparte for $15 million. Although the precise boundaries of the territory were unknown, it stretched west from the Mississippi River to the Rocky Mountains and doubled the land area of the United States. Most important, the Louisiana Purchase opened the Mississippi River to American trade, which had been limited by Spain's control of the river.

Located at the southern end of the Mississippi River, the port city of New Orleans became the crossroads of the American frontier during the first half of the nineteenth century. Thousands of transient American adventurers traveled to and from the city on steamboats, heading for the new towns and settlements rising out of the wilderness along the river. In New Orleans, travelers found a raucous, frontier society where gambling and prostitution were the main recreations. Open tolerance for gambling in New Orleans had originated in the early 1700s with the city's first settlers, the French, who had a passion for card games like *poque*, later known as poker, and *vingt-et-un*, or blackjack. By 1823 New Orleans's leaders had begun to license the first gambling houses in the country. These high-class "palaces of fortune,"[1] as they were called by gamblers, were ornately furnished and kept open day and night. Gamblers could try their luck at the roulette wheel, roll the dice, or play card games like Faro, Monte, poker, and blackjack.

Herbert Asbury, the author of *Sucker's Progress*, describes New Orleans as "the focal point of the gambling fever which began to spread over the United States like a pestilence soon after the American flag had been raised in the Place d'Armes [the city's central square]."[2] The city gave birth to a class of professional gamblers known as sharpers, who headed out into the hinterlands and introduced gambling to the steamboat passengers and settlers along the Mississippi and Ohio Rivers. Sharpers took advantage of wealthy "suckers" who had grown rich in the booming economy of the early nineteenth century. With little experience handling large sums of money, these men often gambled with a recklessness indicative of the frontier's heady spirit of risk and materialism. Asbury maintains that "by the early 1830s between 1,000 and 1,500 professional gamblers more or less regularly worked the steamboats between New Orleans and Louisville . . . where their favorite prey, the rich planter and slave owner and the foolish young scion of a wealthy family, was found in great abundance."[3] Vice districts, where professional gamblers, prostitutes, and assorted rough characters congregated, sprouted in Mississippi River towns like Vicksburg and Natchez. By 1835 gamblers in Vicksburg had cultivated such a bad reputation that the town became the site of the first large-scale vigilante uprising against gamblers and their ilk. The town's successful, albeit temporary, purging of its gambling community was replicated by other southern river communities. As a result, hundreds of professional gamblers scrambled elsewhere in search of more accommodating townsfolk.

Within twenty-five years after the first gambling halls opened for business in New Orleans, similar establishments were "running more or less wide-open in almost every large city of the Union,"[4] according to Asbury. Many of the professional gamblers who had been driven out of the southwest made their way east to fast-growing cities like New York, Baltimore, and Washington, opening lavish gambling palaces based on the New Orleans model. Although ostensibly illegal, eastern gambling halls operated with the tacit approval of politicians, who took a slice of the profits in exchange for looking the other way. In New York alone, it is estimated that thousands of gambling halls operated openly throughout much of the nineteenth century.

During the California gold rush of the late 1840s, New Orleans was the main embarkation point for San Francisco, and gambling made its way to the far western frontier. In *People of Chance: Gambling in American Society from Jamestown to Las Vegas*, author John M. Findlay contends that gold miners were gamblers by nature who had staked their time, energy, and health to come west in search of speedy accumulation. Explains Findlay, "Gold mining stimulated gambling because it encouraged people's trust in luck and speculation."[5] At the height of the gold rush in late 1849, San Francisco was little more than a hastily assembled outpost of forty thousand newly arrived miners and seamen who, outside of gambling, found few recreational diversions. In a "society so loosely knit, and with fortune making and chance taking so highly regarded," Findlay asserts, "gambling flourished."[6] According to *The Annals of San Francisco*, by Frank Soule, John H. Gihon, and James Nisbet, gambling in San Francisco was *"the* amusement—*the* grand occupation of many classes—apparently the life and soul of the place. There were hundreds of gambling saloons in the town."[7]

From 1849 to 1855, the state of California recognized gamblers as professional businessmen, taxing and licensing their gambling operations. But after 1855, with the gold rush in decline and San Francisco growing more established, laws against gambling were enacted. Prohibition was not terribly effective at deterring gamblers, but Findlay maintains that

> the target of reformers was not so much gaming itself as the professional gamblers who made their living from the pastime. Chance taking remained an integral aspect of life in the state, but those who made betting a career were cast out from respectable circles of society because they seemed increasingly incongruous in communities intent on conforming to eastern standards.[8]

The overtly money-grubbing and exploitative characteristics of the frontier gambler were increasingly regarded by well-heeled Californians as a regional embarrassment. Gambling came to be viewed as an unrefined display of base impulses that, as Findlay asserts, "inhibited slow and steady economic growth and compounded the unstable character of the population."[9] Accordingly, professional gamblers in California were tainted as dishonest and in cahoots with corrupt politicians, and gambling's popularity diminished to some degree.

By 1860 San Francisco's freewheeling gambling days were over, but other towns on the western frontier allowed gamblers to ply their trade for many years. From the town's inception in 1859, settlers in Denver, Colorado, patronized dozens of gambling dens. According to Asbury, "Denver retained many of its frontier characteristics for more than half a century, and except for a few brief periods of suppression, was a wide-open gambling town until the early 1920s [although gambling was technically outlawed in 1900]."[10] Kansas City, Missouri; El Paso, Texas; and Santa Fe, New Mexico, were also centers of gambling activity until the late 1800s.

Slowly but surely, though, legalized casino gambling came under attack in the West. The last holdout, Nevada, outlawed gambling in 1910, close on the heels of Arizona and New Mexico, where gambling was banned in 1907 and 1908, respectively. Once again, prohibition arose from pressure on western politicians and residents to conform to eastern standards. Reports of wild, unruly outposts where men could still gamble openly and enjoy concomitant vices like prostitution and heavy drinking did much to raise the ire of puritanical easterners. Back in Washington, D.C., congressmen had demanded that, as a condition for statehood, both Arizona and New Mexico abolish legalized gambling. Arizona congressman Mark Smith had little choice but to comply, but not before firing a few shots at eastern hypocrites. Said Smith in answer to the finger-pointing of a Maine congressman, "I do not wish it understood that I am here in sympathy with gambling, but I do protest against the gentleman from Maine, the farthest point in the United States from my home, coming here to meddle in our quarrels, when, with prohibition in his own State, there are 150 [gambling] saloons open in the town of Bangor, Maine."[11] Of course, gamblers in Bangor had plenty of company on the East Coast. Denizens of cities like New York, who had supposedly tamed their frontier impulses, were still patronizing hundreds of illegal gambling halls at the start of the twentieth century. In the wake of prohibition, western gambling halls followed the eastern example and continued to operate illicitly, moving into the basements of storefronts in cities like Reno, Nevada.

The Return of Legalized Casino Gambling to Nevada

By 1930 card rooms in Gardena, California, and horse racing in Kentucky, New York, and Illinois were the few exceptions to the gambling prohibition that had swept the nation. As the

Great Depression of the 1930s descended, many states faced budget crises due to declining tax revenues. Nevada, an arid and sparsely populated state with a mining-based economy, was struggling. The state's 1910 prohibition against gambling had merely driven a thriving business underground. With liquor prohibition in effect since 1920, gangsters in Chicago, New York, and elsewhere had added gambling to their hugely profitable bootlegging business. As in many western towns, numerous speakeasies and illegal gambling halls were operating tax-free in Reno and Las Vegas, Nevada's largest towns, enriching only criminals. In 1931 Nevada became the first state to reintroduce across-the-board legalization of gambling after more than twenty years of prohibition. Lotteries were the sole exception and were to remain illegal. Other states reconsidered prohibition of gambling as well, and during the 1930s, eighteen states, including California, Texas, Michigan, and Ohio, legalized horse racing. But Nevada would remain the only state with legalized casino gambling for several decades. Findlay alleges that gambling and Nevadans were a natural match since gambling "resembled the chancy pursuit of precious metals . . . and the cyclical patterns of mining encouraged Nevadans to accept lawful gambling."[12] The state also had a history of tolerance for vices shunned in other parts of the country. Before the return of legalized gambling, Nevada had made its name as a state for quickie divorces, requiring a mere six-week residency to qualify, and prostitution was legal in some counties.

For the first few years of gambling legalization, Reno, just over 200 miles to the east of San Francisco, was the state's premier gambling town, but it was rapidly eclipsed by Las Vegas, 450 miles to the south. Once a desolate railroad town, Las Vegas experienced a boom in the early 1930s with the building of the Hoover Dam across the nearby Colorado River. Workers from the project would regularly travel to Las Vegas for gambling. Once the dam was completed in 1935, it became a tourist attraction, and visitors discovered Las Vegas's freewheeling attitude toward gambling and other vices. Explains Findlay, "More than 200,000 visitors combined tours of the Hoover Dam with side trips to the town in 1933. In Las Vegas travelers found a place that seemed at once relaxed and wild. . . . The easy-going nature of the town invited comparison to frontier society, an illusion relished by local boosters."[13] News soon spread of twenty-four-hour gambling in wild Las Vegas—one of the few remaining towns where the risk-taking spirit of the western frontier lived on.

Gambling's Postwar Popularity

By the early 1950s the United States had entered a post–World War II era characterized by economic prosperity and suburban conformity. The threadbare days of the Great Depression were long gone, as was the notion that a risk-driven, frontier society still existed in America. Cities and towns were increasingly similar, dominated by automobiles, look-alike housing developments, and shopping malls selling mass-produced consumer goods. The workplace also became more regimented as large corporations became the primary employers.

In this atmosphere of routine predictability, gambling grew more popular than ever with American thrill seekers. The 1976 Commission on the Review of the National Policy Toward Gambling estimates that "during the 1940s, the public spent . . . $6 billion a year on illegal gambling, more than the combined profits of U.S. Steel, General Motors, General Electric, and the other 100 largest companies."[14] The Las Vegas gambling vacation surfaced in the mid-1950s as a unique way to experience the excitement and risk that had been drained from much of American life. Opening in 1955, the Disneyland amusement park in southern California pioneered a new style of whimsical vacation resort that appealed to the desire of many Americans to temporarily abandon reality. Taking its cue from Disneyland, Las Vegas transformed itself into a theme park for adults. Entrepreneurial gangsters like Benjamin "Bugsy" Siegel and Meyer Lansky opened the first resorts on what became the legendary Las Vegas Strip, a relentless boulevard of lights and sound intended to transport visitors far away from life's routines. The city readily promoted its image as America's Sin City, the only place in the country where people could enjoy the thrill of casino gambling. Explains Julian Halevy in a 1958 article for *Nation* magazine,

> Las Vegas is a very different kind of place from Disneyland, although both seem to me to illustrate a growing need in the United States to escape from reality. . . . Las Vegas deals in

the essence of the American way, narcotizes the number-one preoccupation of daily reality and nightly dream: the Almighty Buck. . . . Disneyland and Las Vegas [both] exist for the relief of tension and boredom. . . . Their huge profits and mushrooming growth suggest that as conformity and adjustment become more rigidly imposed on the American scene, the drift to fantasy release will become a flight.[15]

As Halevy maintains, gambling in Las Vegas cut to the heart of American society. The city reached backed to the frontier ethos of risk and instant attainment, going to great lengths to re-create the thrilling, anything-goes society of the 1800s with a thoroughly modern sheen. By comparison, the workaday drudgery of the outside world appeared stifling, and long-repressed impulses were awakened. Americans were constantly bombarded by cultural messages that placed a premium on materialism and individual wealth, yet the country's puritan streak made people who were too preoccupied with the lure of easy riches feel guilty and crude. Here was a place where openly chasing money was absolutely encouraged. On the Las Vegas Strip, Americans could let go of cultural hypocrisy and take a break from the burden of middle-class virtue, from the strain of pretending that the rewards of hard work, prudent investment, carefully mortgaged futures, and "playing by the rules"—the bedrock of the Protestant work ethic—were worth the effort. Halevy's predictions were correct: The temptations of Las Vegas attracted millions of visitors throughout the 1960s and 1970s, and the city moved to the forefront of American popular culture.

Gambling Is Legalized Around the Country

By the mid-1970s state governments and voters around the country had approved lotteries as a way to fund education, provide property-tax relief, and support programs for senior citizens without raising taxes. Banned by every state since 1894, New Hampshire introduced a lottery sweepstakes in 1964 and was followed by several other states. In addition, the casino gambling industry in Las Vegas, long disparaged as the dominion of organized crime, slowly cleaned up its image. According to Rachel A. Volberg in *When the Chips Are Down: Problem Gambling in America*, "During the late 1960s and 1970s, corporate investors such as Howard Hughes, Kirk Kerkorian, and Merv Griffin, as well as Hilton Hotels, Metro-Goldwyn-Mayer, and Holiday Inns, placed the casino industry on a more legitimate footing."[16] With new credibility, other states finally decided to give casino gambling a try. The New Jersey legislature approved casino gambling for Atlantic City in 1978, imposing strict regulations to ensure that the casinos would be run by corporations, not mobsters. Less than ten years later, the U.S. Supreme Court opened a wide avenue for casino gambling when it ruled in 1987 that Indian tribes were allowed to run gambling operations on reservation lands. Congress outlined the terms under which Indian tribes could negotiate deals with states to run casinos with the Indian Gaming and Regulatory Act of 1988. In the early 1990s Indian casinos began to appear all over the United States. Video poker and card rooms also gained public approval. In the meantime, Las Vegas experienced a boom of unprecedented proportions that attracted record numbers of visitors and recast casino gambling as a harmless recreational activity. In 2003 twenty-nine states had casinos, thirty-seven states had lotteries, and twenty-two had offtrack horse betting. Volberg reports that revenues from legal wagering increased 1,800 percent between 1975 and 1999, exceeding $58 billion.

The Enduring Frontier Spirit, Immigration, and Changing Social Mores

Several factors can be attributed to the American public's widespread acceptance of legalized gambling. First and foremost, the frontier spirit of risk and chance remains a hallmark of American culture. The western frontier is no longer a roughshod land of saloons and sharpers, but it continues to play a significant role in the popular imagination. The American Dream rests on the powerful cultural belief that when life shows little promise, an individual can pull up stakes and begin a better life in a different region of this vast country. Taking a chance on a new town or city is a gamble that comes naturally to millions of Americans, as evidenced by the moving trucks perpetually crossing the continent. Tolerance for gambling is an outgrowth of the cultural attachment to an inexhaustible store of possibility, to the bold assumption that one can head out with just the shirt on his or her back and still hit the jackpot. Incidentally, as of this writing, six thousand Americans each month are choosing to start their lives over in Las Vegas, the nation's gambling capital and fastest-growing city.

Another important factor behind gambling's popularity and legalization is the shifting demographics of the country due to successive waves of immigration. America's first arrivals were Puritans, who disdained chance and gave rise to a largely Protestant nation that remained ashamed and conflicted over gambling, although puritanism was not as prominent on the western frontier. Later arrivals to the United States, like the millions of Irish, Italians, and Jews who landed throughout the nineteenth and early twentieth centuries, held more tolerant attitudes toward gambling. Asserts Steven A. Riess in his book *City Games: The Evolution of American Urban Society and the Rise of Sports*,

> The rapid expansion of [horse racing in the 1920s] owed a great deal to the growing political influence of new immigrants who worked together with the Irish to legalize racetrack gambling. These ethnic groups enjoyed gambling and opposed the efforts of rural WASPs [white Anglo-Saxon Protestants] to exercise social control over their behavior.[17]

With large numbers and growing influence, new immigrants helped to legitimize gambling with urban governments and overcame the prevailing Protestant disapproval for games of chance. More recently, Latinos, Asians, and other groups have dramatically altered the ethnic composition of the nation's largest cities and have exhibited favorable cultural attitudes toward gambling. In their search for a better life, immigrants reinvigorate the risk taking and sense of new possibility that keeps the American Dream alive and from which the activity of gambling naturally emerges.

Finally, social mores have dramatically shifted over the past twenty-five years. In an ever competitive society with a growing disparity between rich and poor, there is no longer a stigma attached to chasing money that is not earned through years of assiduous labor. Daily, millions of Americans purchase lottery tickets, dreaming of instant millions and a life without commutes, bosses, and long hours for low pay. Television game shows like *Who Wants to Be a Millionaire*, *Survivor*, and *Fear Factor* depict middle-class Americans shamelessly competing for huge cash prizes. The vicissitudes of the stock market have also made record numbers of investors aware of the similarities between America's business culture and casino gambling. Although the forces of prohibition may once again target gambling as a destructive force in American popular culture, history illustrates that risk, chance, fierce individualism, and instant gratification—all values inherent to the activity of gambling—may be hardwired into the national character.

Notes

1. Herbert Asbury, *Sucker's Progress: An Informal History of Gambling in America from the Colonies to Canfield.* New York: Dodd, Mead, 1938, p. 113.

2. Asbury, *Sucker's Progress*, p. 109.

3. Asbury, *Sucker's Progress*, p. 204.

4. Asbury, *Sucker's Progress*, p. 113.

5. John M. Findlay, *People of Chance: Gambling in American Society from Jamestown to Las Vegas.* New York: Oxford University Press, 1986, p. 87.

6. Findlay, *People of Chance*, p. 88.

7. Frank Soule, John H. Gihon, and James Nisbet, *The Annals of San Francisco.* New York: D. Appleton, 1854, p. 248.

8. Findlay, *People of Chance*, pp. 95–96.

9. Findlay, *People of Chance*, p. 98.

10. Asbury, *Sucker's Progress*, p. 329.

11. Quoted in Barton Wood Currie, "The Transformation of the Old Southwest," *Century Magazine*, April 1908, p. 905.

12. Findlay, *People of Chance*, p. 118.

13. Findlay, *People of Chance*, pp. 114–15.

14. Commission on the Review of the National Policy Toward Gambling, *Gambling in America.* Washington, DC: U.S. Government Printing Office, 1976, p. 46.

15. Julian Halevy, "Disneyland and Las Vegas," *Nation*, June 7, 1958, pp. 511, 513.

16. Rachel A. Volberg, *When the Chips Are Down: Problem Gambling in America.* New York: Century Foundation, 2001, p. 25.

17. Steven A. Riess, *City Games: The Evolution of American Urban Society and the Rise of Sports.* Urbana: University of Illinois Press, 1989, pp. 187–88.

EXAMINING POP CULTURE

Gambling's Hold on American Culture

Luck vs. the Protestant Work Ethic

Jackson Lears

The United States is a nation founded by Puritans who believed that God would reward men and women who worked hard with prosperity and affluence. The Protestant work ethic—the belief that anyone, regardless of background, can become a "self-made" success by working diligently toward his or her goals—has embedded itself in American culture. Because gambling is an activity that favors luck over work, it has regularly been labeled a vice that undermines principal American values.

In the following essay, Jackson Lears examines the rising tension between luck and the Protestant work ethic in American culture as legalized gambling has spread to nearly every corner of the country. The author contends that gambling's critics overlook the fact that the United States was founded by risk-taking colonists and thrives on a capitalist system centered around chance. Gambling is popular because it allows participants to embrace the "power of luck" that is regularly disparaged in America and momentarily break free of oppressive moral convention, in the author's opinion. Lears is the author of *Something for Nothing: Luck in America*, from which this excerpt is taken.

■

THE IMPULSE TO GAMBLE IS MYSTERIOUS AND powerful. Anyone who doubts it might consider a few scenes from the recent casino revival: In Connecticut, a couple leaves a nine-year-old boy in a car overnight in freezing weather while they gamble at Foxwoods Casino. In Mississippi, parents also leave their twelve-year-old son in a vehicle, but with a revolver for protection. In Niagara Falls, casino operators complain that slot machine players are urinating into the plastic coin cups supplied by the casino or onto the floor beside the machines. Some wear adult diapers. All are reluctant to leave a machine they are hoping will soon pay off. And in Louisiana, video poker players report trancelike out-of-body experiences, the feeling of "being sucked into oblivion."

Virtue vs. Vice

What is going on here? For many public moralists, the answer is simple. According to [journalist] Walter Cronkite, the legalization of gambling means that "a nation once built on a work ethic embraces the belief that it's possible to get something for nothing." Similar sentiments have sparked nationwide campaigns against casinos, one led by a Methodist minister and Vietnam veteran named Thomas Grey. He calls his recruits "Gideon's Army" and claims to be "fighting a battle for the soul of America."

This struggle is not uniquely American. Gambling is provoking ferocious controversy in other countries as well. In 1992 Chinese Communist officials in Shanghai unleashed a campaign against mah-jongg that included mass self-criticisms by 4300 party members who had sworn off gambling, the public burning of 400 mah-jongg sets, and the commissioning of 5000 antigambling squads. None of this stemmed the Chinese obsession with the game. The modern conflict over gambling is part of a global war that has erupted periodically for several centuries—the clash between revolutionary virtue and reactionary vice. That struggle has surfaced whenever the righteous declare their intention to remake the licentious, to create a systematically disciplined "new man." As Michael Walzer once observed, there is a direct lineage from Cromwell to Lenin. And rectitudinous modernizers, whether Puritans or Communists, have never had much truck with gambling.

From the modernizers' view, gambling was a relic of a decadent old regime—a vice that epitomized the European haut monde [high society] evoked by [novelist Fyodor] Dostoevsky in *The Gambler* (1866). Dostoevsky's Roulettenburg is a society powered by feverish, erotic obsession—with money, status, romantic attachment. Whatever the object, what is crucial is the desire to be always in pursuit, on the edge, whether at the roulette tables or in a lady's chamber. The only constraints on this quest for intense experience are the remnants of a creaking caste tradition, a set of musty principles and rituals that easily can be counterfeited. In Roulettenburg, it is always an open question whether this marquis or that countess is the genuine article or not. In contrast, the revolutionary "new man"—bourgeois or socialist—was an icon of authenticity.

Fault Lines

Still, despite the international dimensions of controversy over gambling, the recurrent furor has a peculiarly American resonance. Debate about gambling reveals fundamental fault lines in American character, sharp tensions between an impulse toward risk and a zeal for control. Those tensions may be universal, but seldom have they been so sharply opposed as in the United States, where longings for a lucky strike have been counterbalanced by a secular Protestant Ethic that has questioned the very existence of luck. . . . Contemporary gambling games recall ancient rituals—attempts to divine the decrees of fate, and conjure the wayward force of luck. Those rituals were (and are) rooted in a distinctive world view, based on a certain respect—even reverence—for chance. This outlook contrasted sharply with what became an American creed: the faith that we can master chance through force of will, and that rewards will match merits in this world as well as the next. For me, writing about luck is a way of eavesdropping on a contentious conversation at the core of our culture—a conversation that raises fundamental ethical, philosophical, and even religious issues.

What makes the conversation so revealing is that it counterposes two distinct accounts of American character. One narrative puts the big gamble at the center of American life: from the earliest English settlements at Jamestown and Massachusetts Bay, risky ventures in real estate (and other less palpable commodities) power the progress of a fluid, mobile democracy. The speculative confidence man is the hero of this tale—the man (almost always he is male) with his eye on the Main Chance rather than the Moral Imperative. The other narrative exalts a different sort of hero—a disciplined self-made man, whose success comes through careful cultivation of (implicitly Protestant) virtues in cooperation with a Providential plan. The first account implies a contingent universe where luck matters and admits that net worth may have nothing to do with moral worth. The second assumes a coherent universe where earthly rewards match ethical merits and suggests that Providence has ordered this world as well as the next.

The self-made man has proven to be a far more influential culture hero than the confidence man. The secular version of Providence has resonated with some characteristically American presumptions. A providential sense of destiny could be expanded from individuals to groups and ultimately to nations—and to none more easily than the United States. Even before there was a United States, colonial orators assumed their settlements would play a redemptive role in the sacred drama of world history. As the Puritan John Winthrop declared in 1630, the holy commonwealth at Massachusetts Bay would be a "Citty on a Hille," a beacon of inspiration for all Christendom. By the revolutionary era, the city on a hill had spread to the whole society: America became "God's New Israel." As the new nation grew richer and more powerful during the nineteenth century, the profounder religious meanings of Providence began to fall away. Prosperity itself came to seem a sign of God's blessing—at least to the more affluent, who have always felt drawn to secular notions of Providence. Like the Rockefellers and other prominent pewholders in Protestant churches, America was rich because it deserved to be. For the deserving nation as for the deserving individual, progress was inevitable. Or so the more fortunate have assumed, from the first Gilded Age to our own more recent one.

Denying Chance, Disdain for Gambling

A providentially ordered society contained little space for gamblers—at least in its conventional morality. Yet it was precisely the pervasiveness of social uncertainty that made the insistence on moral certainty so necessary. The salience of secular providence rose in response to the comparative openness of American society. Fortunate people have always wanted to believe that they deserved their good fortune, but fortunate Americans were in especially urgent need of reassurance. Compared to the Old World, the United States was a riot of shape-shifting status strivers. Beginning in colonial times, the abolition of hereditary privilege broadened opportunities for counterfeiting profitable selves. Main Chances multiplied with the emergence of unregulated market society in the early nineteenth century. As in Dostoevsky's Roulettenburg, impostors proliferated, and the very boundlessness of American possibility demanded a stricter set of internal prohibitions than were available in aristocratic old Europe. The exorcism of the confidence man required the invocation of his double, the self-made man.

As the apotheosis of plodding diligence, the cult of self-made manhood has posed severe challenges to American gamblers. For more than two centuries, our moralists and success mythologists have disdained gambling and denied chance, arguing that "you make your own luck" and insisting on a solid link between merit and reward. The *New York Times* columnist William Safire echoes generations of clerical critics in his bitter condemnations of legalized gambling. "The truth is that nothing is for nothing," he writes. "Hard work, talent, merit, will win you something. Reliance on luck, playing the sucker, will make you a loser all your life." In a competitive society, few apparitions are more terrifying than the specter of "the loser"— the poor sap who never really grasps how to play the game.

Yet the defenders of diligence have never entirely vanquished the devotees of chance. At least since Alexis de Tocqueville [French historian and author of the 1835 book *Of Democracy in America*] compared American society to "a vast lottery," our business mythology has celebrated risk-taking, knowing when to hold and when to fold, taking advantage of "the breaks." Especially in flush times, it has not always been easy to distinguish gambling from speculation or investment, and even Horatio Alger [nineteenth-century author of self-help books] knew that luck was as important as pluck in achieving success. The gambler, endlessly starting over with every hand of cards, has embodied the American metaphysic of reinventing the self, reawakening possibilities from one moment to the next. The gambler and the entrepreneur have been twinned.

The Perfect Target

Still it has been crucial to tell them apart. For those who believed that the American economic system was part of a providential order, the respectable businessman could never be reduced to merely a fortunate gambler. Illicit gambling had to be distinguished from shrewd investing and successful entrepreneurship. Historically, Safire and other moralists have played a crucial role in legitimating market culture, explaining away random or rigged inequalities by incantatory references to hard work and just deserts.

For a while, in recent years, it looked as if the bull market of the 1990s had posed a fundamental challenge to this rhetorical tradition. The sorcerers of the dot-com economy temporarily severed stock prices from the ballast of company earnings—the product of disciplined achievement over time. By banishing that vestige of the Protestant Ethic, they also helped to create new models of legitimate gambling. The best-known were day traders—sitting entranced at their computer consoles, dodging bullets, riding momentum, selling out just in time (they hoped), and feeling drawn inexorably to the frisson of danger. Their solitary, obsessive existence bore a striking resemblance to the life of the compulsive gambler.

Yet descriptions of day trading remained largely untainted by the language of pathology. It was a risky business, economic pundits agreed, but at the same time merely a distilled version of the game we were all constantly being urged to play. When money seemed magically to beget more money—or make it disappear—with no more apparent rhyme or reason than the arrangement of numbers on a screen, the hallowed distinction between gambling and investment became more difficult than ever to sustain.

All the more reason, then, to legitimate the new, on-line gamblers by stigmatizing the old, off-line ones, who tend to be grayer, paunchier, and poorer than the young whippets of Wall Street and Silicon Valley. Stock trading may breed pathological or destructive behavior, but it is seldom subjected to the clinical gaze of psychiatry—and even more rarely, in recent years, to the baleful stare of moralists. Even now, when we know that much of the bull market prosperity was based on fraud, moral outrage tends to focus on the confidence men who rigged the game rather than the game itself. As official thought leaders squirm to protect investor confidence, stock trading preserves a precarious legitimacy. Gambling, in contrast, remains a perfect target for dissection, disapproval, and oversimplification.

A Narrow Critique

Though attitudes toward gambling reveal complexities at the core of our culture, inquiry into its significance has remained largely within the censorious boundaries suggested by a *New York Times* headline: "Fervid Debate on Gambling: Disease or Moral Weakness?" This puritanism has long framed American discussion of personal habits that undermine the (implicitly Protestant) ethos of systematic self-control: cigarettes, alcohol, drugs, idiosyncratic sexual tastes. With respect to gambling, as with other guilty pleasures, we are offered a non-choice between moral and medical idioms of disapproval.

The tendency to view gambling only in the context of other associated vices (alcoholism, drug addiction, prostitution) has clouded our understanding of its larger cultural meanings. A reformist agenda of social control provides a lens too limited to capture the complexity of practices rooted in venerable traditions. The problem with the critique of gambling is not that it is mistaken—without question, compulsive gamblers have ruined legions of lives, not least their own—but that it is too narrowly circumscribed. By reducing gambling to a collection of psychiatric symptoms or a sign of political corruption, critics have overlooked its wider web of connections to ancient, multifaceted rituals that have addressed profound human needs and purposes.

Debate about gambling is never just about gambling: it is about different ways of being in the world. . . . The main narrative concerns the constantly shifting tensions between rivalrous American cultures of chance and control. At its most familiar moments, this tale involves the face-off between the confidence man, the devotee of Fortuna, and the self-made man, the herald of Providence. But the story raises more serious philosophical issues than that confrontation suggests. It also ranges more widely, including women as well as men, conjurers and their clients as well as faro dealers and their dupes.

The Culture of Chance

The confidence man is only a recent and commercial representative of an ancient, capacious culture of chance—a culture more at ease with randomness and irrationality, more doubtful that diligence is the only path to success, than our dominant culture of control. The culture of chance acquired special significance in the American setting, where it met unprecedented opposition from Protestant and later managerial apostles of self-discipline. But its origins can be traced into the dim past, to the person who first cast stones or shells to read in their chance array the will of the cosmos—and perhaps to conjure its power in his own or his clients' behalf. Runes are the ancestors of cards and dice. The conjurer and the gambler are kinfolk under the skin.

Cultures of chance and control are ideals that overlap and intermingle. They rarely exist in pure form. While both seek patterns of meaning in the random chaos of human events, what varies is the role of chance in this project. Cultures of control—as in the American Protestant or managerial tradition—dismiss chance as a demon to be denied or a difficulty to be minimized; while cultures of chance treat it as a source of knowledge and a portal of possibility. Cultures of chance have their own rituals, beliefs, even gods (though ones largely unacknowledged). They also have their own fetishes. A glance at the baroque extravagance of slot machine design leaves little doubt that the one-armed bandit is a fetish object refashioned for a modern industrial age.

Whatever their forms and rituals, cultures of chance encourage reverence for grace, luck, and fortune—powers beyond human mastery whose favor may nonetheless be courted. . . . By luck or fortune, I mean the force at the core of the cosmos that governs chance events, that can be sometimes conjured but never coerced. Grace is even more elusive. It is what happens when openness to chance yields a deeper awareness of the cosmos or one's place in it—when luck leads to spiritual insight.

The gods of the culture of chance survive in the contemporary American setting. The woman who consults a dream book to interpret her unconscious life (and learn what number to play) may be participating in an ancient tradition of divination. The man who buys a lottery ticket may be paying homage to Fortuna, a deity long discredited by devotees of self-help. However futile, his gesture still loosens the keystone of the dominant culture of control: our quasi-official faith (evangelical or managerial) in the human capacity to master fate. Apparently trivial games can become ways of raising ultimate questions—of connecting numbers running and cosmology, gambling and grace.

Outside Christian tradition, grace could appear in many secular forms. It could serve as a term for that ever-elusive sense of oneness with the cosmos that athletes experience when they are "in the zone," artists when they are compelled by inspiration, or gamblers when they are on a hot streak. If we are lucky, grace could be what happens when we take a chance, when we cease trying to control events and simply play.

In *Homo Ludens* (1938), the Dutch historian Johan Huizinga identified "the play element in culture," demonstrating how a spirit of serious play animated religion, philosophy, law, war, and a host of other human activities—a spirit obscured but not obliterated by the modern obsession with systematic work. The spirit of serious play preserves a critical edge, despite its alarming resemblance to pop-psychological cant about the wisdom of recovering our "inner child." The key to its complexity is the constant possibility (and perhaps the ultimate certainty) of loss.

Challenging the Success Mythology

For the gambler as for the believer, grace can be born of losing as well as of winning. According to the fictional female gambler in Peter Carey's *Oscar and Lucinda*, there was always the chance that "one could experience that lovely, lightheaded feeling of loss, the knowledge that one had abandoned one more brick from the foundation of one's fortune, that one's purse was quite, quite empty . . . and no matter what panic and remorse all this would produce on the morrow, one had in those moments of loss such an immense feeling of relief—

there was no responsibility, no choice."

In a society such as ours, where responsibility and choice are exalted, where capital accumulation is a duty and cash a sacred cow, what could be more subversive than the readiness to reduce money to mere counters in a game? The gambler's willingness to throw it all away with merely a shrug of the shoulders could embody a challenge, implicit but powerful, to the modern utopian fantasy of the systematically productive life. The idea that loss is not only inescapable but perhaps even liberating does not sit well with our success mythology, which assumes at least implicitly that "winning is the only thing."

What is sorely missing from American public debate is a sense, historical and spiritual, of this connection between gambling and grace. How could it not be? Urgent policy decisions regarding the prohibition of video poker or the providing of tax breaks for casino owners can hardly await the outcome of metaphysical speculation. Still the larger questions—the ultimate questions—demand consideration. Occasionally they have received it. The maverick psychoanalyst Theodor Reik, for example, called gambling "a kind of question addressed to destiny"— aptly catching the religious motives behind the wagering impulse. But the crucial, clarifying connection between casinos and churches is the link between gambling and grace. The notion of grace as a kind of spiritual luck, a free gift from God, lies at the heart of gambling's larger cultural significance. . . .

A Rigid Culture of Control

A culture less intent on the individual's responsibility to master destiny might be more capacious, more generous, more gracious. A recognition of the power of luck might encourage fortunate people to imagine their own misfortune and transcend the arrogance of the meritocratic myth—to acknowledge how fitfully and unpredictably people get what they deserve. So at least we can hope.

But that sort of openness is in short supply in the contemporary United States. Ideals of order and system, productivity and predictability, dominate our daily lives. In private affairs, the culture of control has made the harried look a sign of success—or at least of full participation in society. Sensible strivers and their children compete for an empty (and unattainable) goal of "peak performance" in everything from sports and sex to standardized testing. Genuine leisure languishes. Possibilities for play evaporate in a utilitarian atmosphere.

The culture of control continues to sustain the smug, secular version of Christian providentialism that has framed American morality for two centuries, though the favored idiom is now technocratic rather than religious. The hubris of the providential view lies in its tendency to sanctify the secular; in its glib assurance not merely that we are all part of a divine— or "evolutionary"—plan, but also that we can actually see that plan at work in prevailing social and economic arrangements, even in the outcomes of global power struggles. A more chastened (and realistic) perspective might grant a greater role to chance, if only as a counterpoint to the arrogance of ultimate explanation. That perspective is tricky to reconstruct, but it can be located in the speculations of artists and intellectuals, the assumptions of idiosyncratic believers and marginal subcultures, and the vernacular philosophy of gamblers.

All these groups are well positioned to challenge the central dogma of our time: the idea that money is an indicator of fundamental value. But none is better positioned than gamblers. "Great gamblers have seen the grim absurdities in capital and its accumulation," David Thomson [author of *In Nevada*] reports from Nevada. "They know money is merely a game (like 10,000 on the Dow) and they insist on being playful with it. There is ease and even transcendence in that feeling." Viewed from Thomson's angle of vision, Las Vegas might lay claim to a more than metaphorically religious significance. The city is, he writes, "that rare thing: a city built in the spirit that knows its days are numbered. That's the eerie spirit of its profound casualness. The house itself knows that it is only there by the grace of God." An emphasis on the precariousness of wealth, the impermanence of life, and the arbitrariness of money as a measure of worth—if these are tenets of a gambler's worldview, it may be a perspective worth cultivating.

Even among gamblers, the desire for something for nothing is more than mere laziness and greed; it often involves a longing to transcend the realm of money-worship altogether. In his *Memoir of a Gambler* (1979), the playwright Jack Richardson acknowledged that the gambler (or at least the one he knew best) was engaged in a theodicy—in an effort to glimpse some coherence in the cosmos. To the "old voices" in his head demanding that he justify his life as a gambler, Richardson replied: "I want to know. . . . I want finally to know. . . . Whether I am to have any grace in this life."

Escaping Moral Convention

Such vast longings may well remain unfulfilled, at the gaming table as well as at the Communion table. Usually the best the gambler can hope for is a reminder that in spite of all the talk about making your own luck, good luck still happens on its own terms—obeying its own mysterious (or nonexistent) laws, without regard for the merits or demerits of the lucky person. But it does happen, at least from time to time. And when it does, it brings a dizzying sense of release from the grip of moral convention. As Frederick and Steven Barthelme recall in their remarkable memoir of gambling and loss, a big win at the casino was "a victory over money, the tyrant that has been pushing you around your whole life," and it was also something more. "There is a perfect alignment or echo between our experience in gambling and our experience in the world, and it is in the big win . . . that the echo is most apparent. All the disorder, illogic, injustice, and pointlessness that we have spent our ordinary days ignoring or denying, pretending to see the same world our fellow citizens insist on seeing, trying to go along to get along, trying not to think too much about the implications, all of it flows forth in this confirmation of pointlessness—by luck."

Watching those funny little symbols fall into place, the ones that resemble turtles and that represent a thousand dollars each, the jackpot winner knows better than any Sartrean the absurdity of life. "It's about beating *logic*," the Barthelmes observe. "It's about chance confirming everything you knew but could make no place for in your life." To court grace, luck, and fortune through serious play is to circumvent what passes for common sense and seek to spring the trap of the predictable. What happens next remains to be seen.

Gambling's Massive Expansion

Timothy L. O'Brien

Major forms of legalized gambling—casinos, card rooms, state lotteries, horse betting, and video poker—have spread from the confines of Nevada and a handful of other states to every state in the union with the exception of Hawaii and Utah. The massive expansion of legalized gambling in the United States began in the mid-1970s as state governments capitalized on the public's growing tolerance and voracious appetite for games of chance.

Timothy L. O'Brien is a reporter for the *New York Times* and the author of *Bad Bet: The Inside Story of the Glamour, Glitz, and Danger of America's Gambling Industry*. The following excerpt from *Bad Bet* describes how gambling has become a ubiquitous pastime in America, attracting more of the public's recreation dollars than baseball, the movies, and Disneyland combined. The author contends that many of the negative impacts of gambling, from failed economic benefits to problem gamblers, have been dismissed by the gambling industry in its push to peddle instant gratification. Its detractors notwithstanding, widespread gambling is unlikely to disappear because Americans simply love to gamble, in O'Brien's opinion.

AT ALMOST ANY MINUTE OF ANY HOUR OF ANY day in some corner of the country, a gambler, lit from within by a desire to strike it rich, drops a quarter through a narrow slit into a squat 200-pound slot machine.

■

Playing the Slots

The quarter, a copper wafer sandwiched by thin layers of nickel and weighing less than six grams, falls a couple of inches inside the machine into a small metal detector called a comparitor. To ensure that the coin isn't a counterfeit, the comparitor instantly scans it for weight and content against another quarter permanently lodged in the machine. From there, the quarter continues its brief descent past several optical sensors that measure the coin's motion, searching in milliseconds for any odd movements that might indicate a cheater is tampering with the machine. Finally, ushered with approval through the comparitor, the quarter plunges downward, breaking a thin beam of light emitted by yet another scanner and producing an electronic pulse that prepares the machine for action. The quarter, its mission complete, ends its journey in a large hopper in the bottom of the machine, joining as many as 999 other coins that have preceded it.

Our player then presses a button or pulls the machine's handle, triggering another electronic pulse that tells a computer chip deep inside the machine that the game has begun. Following the chip's command, a computer program randomly generates a number that determines where and when the machine's reels will stop, whether the reel combination is a winner or loser, and, if it's a winner, how big the payout will be. The machines are programmed to pay out small amounts frequently, to attract bettors who prefer repeated stroking, or to pay out larger amounts intermittently, to attract bettors who want to feel like they've really cashed in. Our player, like most slot players, will probably lose far more than she ever takes out of the machine. In return, she may experience those few seconds of adrenaline, sexual joy that course through the body whenever the machine, in its benevolence, scoops a bouquet of quarters out of the hopper and plops them into what the gambling industry delicately terms a loud bowl—a steel tray that permits a longer, noisier drop of coins on the payout. A noisy payout is essential, for it firmly reminds the player, and all those around her, that money does, in fact, talk.

Faceless, gleaming, and the bearers of dreams in late-twentieth-century America, slot machines have helped fuel the most massive expansion of gambling in U.S. history. Institutionalized in an unprecedented fashion, an ancient and unruly activity has become one of the most ubiquitous and well-marketed pastimes in America. And the torrent of cash that spews from our pockets and streams through the corporate board-rooms and darker corners of America's gambling establishment has created a commercial juggernaut. In 1976, we bet $17.3 billion legally. In 1996, we bet $586.5 billion. We lost $47.6 billion gambling legally in 1996, about $14 billion more than New York City's public budget and more than twice as much as the Coca-Cola Company's sales in the same year. Judged by dollars spent, gambling is now more popular in America than baseball, the movies, and Disneyland—*combined*.

We bet in casinos and at the racetrack; we bet on football and basketball games, and we bet on state lotteries and the stock market; we bet in our churches and in our synagogues, and we bet in our offices and in our homes. Yet, as entrenched as gambling always has been in American life, its raptures and demons have never been so easily accessible as they are right now. Social taboos and laws that once confined gambling's availability have been cast aside in a national rush to embrace this most dangerous of games. Some communities, most notably the Mississippi Gulf Coast and some Native American reservations, have been rejuvenated by commercial gambling's recent expansion. Still other places, such as New Orleans and Atlantic City, offer stark reminders of how little gambling can deliver when called upon to be an economic savior. But the siren continues to enchant, because commercial gambling's strongest appeal is to the desperate—to small towns and cities beaten into economic submission; to states stripped of federal tax support and angling for ways to plug holes in their budgets; to Native Americans banished to the outer rim of society; to senior citizens hungry for a sense of belonging and stimulation; and to a minority of gamblers so vulnerable that they will do whatever it takes to keep feeding their habits. All are drawn by the hope that the tug of a slot machine's handle or a roll of the dice will transform them.

Dependence on Problem Gamblers

The large corporations that have taken over casinos from the mobsters and outcasts who once dominated the industry are quick to take exception to this portrait. They insist that they are in the entertainment business. Desperation is not part of their vocabulary. Supported by well-oiled public relations machinery, an armada of political lobbyists, and increasingly friendly legislators, gambling companies contend that most people wager to briefly escape the grind of a workaday world. And this is true. Most gamblers bet within their budgets and treat a weekend in Las Vegas as just another social outing. But there is a little secret lurking behind this truth: the gambling industry's financial well-being depends on a small, hardcore group of regulars, many of whom are compulsive or problem gamblers. Interviews with casino executives and managers indicate that in most markets the bulk of gambling revenue, as much as 80 percent, comes from a small percentage of gamblers, about 20 percent. The precise extent to which the gambling industry's fortunes rely on compulsive or problem gamblers awaits a thorough statistical analysis. Raw data that would make such a study meaningful lie buried in casino companies' marketing departments. Until recently, the industry has been loath to examine its dependence on compulsive and problem gamblers, because an honest discussion of the matter reveals that the most loyal casino patrons aren't, in the argot of gambling's new retailspeak, simply "customers." Many of them are marks. Viewed in this light, compulsive bettors confront the gambling business with the same threats and challenges that nicotine addiction posed for the tobacco industry. And, like their counterparts in the tobacco industry, gambling executives have spent decades dismissing or ignoring the grim realities at the core of their business.

Of course, wagering in America is about much more than the ravaging of compulsive gamblers, because most bettors gamble for more complex reasons than desperation. The sports world, utterly dependent on the interest gambling generates among its fans, attracts some of the most cerebral bettors in the country, those anxious to match wits with oddsmakers and bookies. A similar breed of gambler inhabits the stock market, where the molten core of the American financial system is at once uniquely innovative and a cauldron of potentially destabilizing speculation.

But it is in the throbbing environment of casinos, and in

the more mundane workings of state lotteries, that modern gambling's goals are most blatantly on display. Commercial gambling interests are forever ratcheting up the tempo of their offerings, introducing games and products designed to be played quickly, repetitively, and with a minimum of thought. As the gambling industry becomes more skilled at peddling instant gratification, slower, less frenetic forums for betting, such as racetracks and bingo halls, have been eclipsed. Speed sells. And it can be sold anywhere, for with the advent of on-line wagering, commercial gambling has, quite literally, entered the bedroom.

So appealing is the cozy prospect of home and hearth that resorts such as Las Vegas have tried, though with only limited success, to repackage themselves as family destinations replete with theme parks and other child-friendly attractions. To beckon the kiddies further, casinos have installed video arcades and day-care centers. Visits to casinos often reveal flocks of adolescents hovering on the periphery of these decidedly adult playgrounds. It is only when tragedy strikes—as it did in early 1997, when a seven-year-old girl was raped and murdered in the bathroom of a Nevada casino—that the propriety of reeling children into the orbit of casinos is questioned. Even so, studies suggest that gambling among children and teenagers has matched legalized gambling's growth, with many children exhibiting all the psychological wounds and social warts of compulsives.

For the Love of Gambling

Gambling's expansion during the last decade [1990s] has been greeted with mounting apprehension and criticism. The most potent come from Christian activists, who bear a striking resemblance to the temperance crusaders who have popped up at various junctures in American history. Moral high-mindedness and human desire have a way of butting heads, and there is nothing like a little bit of vice to stir up a good fight in America. But while there are good reasons to be wary of gambling, there are very few reasons to believe that either the impulse or the activity will disappear anytime soon.

We gamble despite the fact that we know the odds are strongly against us.

We gamble despite the fact that it rarely funds passage out of an eroding middle-class existence once heralded as a bulwark of our society.

We gamble despite the fact that the casino industry only sporadically meets its promise of economic deliverance for sagging communities and cash-strapped states.

We gamble despite the fact that gambling occasionally destroys lives.

We gamble because we can't help ourselves.

We love it.

America's New Gamblers

Rachel A. Volberg

Rachel A. Volberg is the author of *When the Chips Are Down: Problem Gambling in America*, from which the following analysis of gambling participation trends in the United States is excerpted. According to Volberg, middle-class Americans have steadily increased their gambling activity over the past twenty-five years, a trend that mirrors the expansion of gambling from casinos to bars, convenience stores, and other places where it had never been available. These new gamblers span all age groups and races and include nearly equal numbers of men and women. Nonetheless, prevailing attitudes toward gambling remain complex, with many Americans expressing strong reservations about the spread of legalized gambling, despite their tendency to gamble. In the author's opinion, gambling may decline in popularity over time as the public learns to balance work and family commitments with easy access to gambling. However, the rise of Internet gambling is likely to open a new avenue for the industry's growth.

GAMBLING AMONG THE UPPER CLASSES, WHETHER on horses, cards, casino games, real estate, or stocks, has long been condoned in most Western societies. Despite the efforts of reformers, similar activities have been broadly tolerated among the working and lower classes. In contrast, until the latter part of the twentieth century, gambling among the middle classes was widely discouraged. Over a decade ago, John Rose-

■

crance [author of the 1998 book *Gambling Without Guilt: The Legitimation of an American Pastime*] argued that the rapid legalization of gambling would lead to growth in the gambling participation of the middle classes. Given the size and influence of the middle class in American society, Rosecrance believed that their acceptance of legal gambling would be an important factor in the continued expansion of lotteries, casinos, and pari-mutuel wagering in the United States. The results of the two national studies of gambling that have been carried out in the United States are evidence that Rosecrance was correct.

Rising Participation in Lotteries and Casinos

The first survey was done by the Institute for Social Research at the University of Michigan in 1975 on behalf of the Commission on the Review of the National Policy Toward Gambling. The second was carried out by the National Opinion Research Center at the University of Chicago in 1998 on behalf of the National Gambling Impact Study Commission. Although the 1975 and 1998 surveys used somewhat different methodologies, they were sufficiently similar to enable some comparisons to be made.

While there was substantial social acceptance of gambling long before most Americans had access to legal gambling opportunities, gambling participation has increased as access has grown. A Gallup poll in 1950 estimated that 57 percent of the American population had gambled at least once. In 1975, the first national survey of gambling in the United States showed that 68 percent of adults had gambled at some point in their lives; the second national survey in 1998 found that 86 percent of adults had done so.

In contrast to lifetime participation, past-year gambling participation rates have not changed much since 1975. The proportion of respondents in the two national surveys indicating that they had gambled in the past year barely changed between 1975 and 1998, rising from 61 percent to 63 percent. Americans in 1998 were far more likely to participate in casino and lottery gambling, which are widely advertised and highly visible, and much less likely to participate in older types of gambling with less visibility, such as bingo and horse race wagering. In 1998, the percentage of people who reported playing the lottery in the past year was two times the percentage in 1975, while the increase in the percentage of respondents who reported gambling in a casino in the past year was even greater. In contrast, past-year bingo participation and past-year participation in horse race wagering both decreased by two-thirds between 1975 and 1998.

Gender and Gambling

In 1975, the types and amount of gambling done by men and women were quite different. The 1975 national survey found that 68 percent of males and 55 percent of females participated in all types of gambling. As the availability of legal gambling has grown in America, however, women's gambling has started to look more like the gambling done by men. Table 1 shows

Table 1. Lifetime, Past-Year, and Weekly Gambling by Gender, Age, and Ethnicity (%)

	Ever	Past year	Weekly
Total	85.6	63.3	16.3
Male	88.1	67.6	20.9
Female	83.2	59.3	12.0
18–29	83.7	65.2	11.8
30–39	87.5	66.2	15.7
40–49	90.2	66.6	15.5
50–64	86.1	65.7	21.4
65+	79.8	50.0	18.9
White	87.5	65.1	15.4
Black	77.7	56.4	22.3
Other	83.1	60.4	15.4

Source: Gambling Impact and Behavior Survey, Public Use File, data available through the Inter-University Consortium for Political and Social Research at the University of Michigan, available at http://www.icpsr.umich.edu/SAMHDA/fasttrack.html.

that while men still gamble more than women, the difference between the genders has narrowed to only a few percentage points. As Table 2 illustrates, past-year casino and lottery players are just as likely to be women as men.

In contrast to legal forms, women are far less likely than men to participate in *illegal* types of gambling. In 1975, 17 percent of males and only 5 percent of females participated in illegal types of gambling. In 1998, men were still more likely than women to engage in illegal forms of gambling—men in the 1998 survey were significantly more likely than women to gamble in card rooms and at unlicensed gambling establishments and to participate in private wagers among themselves. The only type of gambling that women are more likely than men to participate in is bingo.

As with illegal gambling, the scope of women's gambling—that is, the number of gambling activities in which they participate—is more limited than that of men. A 1989 telephone survey of Iowa adults found that while women were not significantly different from men in the frequency of their gambling, the amounts they wagered, or the time they spent gambling, they engaged in significantly fewer gambling activities than men. An analysis of gambling participation among citizens of four states surveyed between 1992 and 1994 also found that women were less likely to participate in multiple gambling domains than men.

Age, Ethnicity, and Gambling

Together, age and gender are the strongest demographic predictors of participation in specific types of gambling. Like the gambling of women compared with men, older Americans are less likely than younger Americans to gamble. Furthermore, when older Americans do gamble, they tend to be involved in fewer activities than younger Americans.

The 1998 national survey found that while lifetime gambling participation had increased for all age groups since 1975, the increase was far more dramatic for older adults than for younger adults. In contrast to lifetime gambling, past-year gambling participation actually decreased among young adults, but it increased among adults ages 45 to 64 and doubled among persons ages 65 and over. In spite of this increase,

Table 2. Past-Year Gambling Participation by Gender, Age, and Ethnicity (%)

	Male	Female	18–29	30–39	40–49	50–64	65+	White	Black	Other
Casino	27.0	24.4	25.6	26.2	26.3	31.5	17.8	26.1	24.0	24.6
Track	9.5	6.8	8.2	7.1	8.8	9.5	7.2	8.2	7.9	7.6
Lottery	55.3	47.9	49.1	55.7	56.2	55.8	38.5	52.4	47.7	49.7
Bingo	3.0	6.8	6.3	4.8	3.8	5.3	4.8	4.8	3.3	7.6
Charitable	4.6	4.3	3.9	4.4	4.1	6.5	3.3	5.3	1.1	2.8
Card rooms	3.2	0.5	3.9	1.6	1.2	1.6	0.4	2.2	0.8	1.0
Private	14.4	5.7	18.2	10.6	7.0	6.9	4.1	10.9	4.4	9.8
Store	10.1	5.7	9.4	9.3	6.9	9.7	2.8	8.9	5.7	4.0
Unlicensed	9.8	5.7	10.5	8.0	9.1	7.1	2.2	9.0	3.3	4.8
Indian	7.1	5.8	6.0	7.8	4.6	8.9	4.3	7.5	1.9	4.3

Source: Gambling Impact and Behavior Survey, Public Use File, data available through the Inter-University Consortium for Political and Social Research at the University of Michigan, available at http://www.icpsr.umich.edu/SAMHDA/fasttrack.html.

seniors are still underrepresented in the total population of past-year gamblers.

The picture becomes more complicated when we examine the types of gambling in which people of different ages are likely to participate. As Table 2 shows, with only a few exceptions, past-year participation in specific types of gambling is highest among adults ages 30 to 64 and lowest among adults ages 65 and over. Adults ages 50 to 64 are substantially more likely than individuals in other age groups to have engaged in charitable gambling and to have gambled at an Indian casino or bingo hall. In contrast, adults ages 18 to 29 are substantially more likely than older adults to have gambled privately. Adults ages 65 and over are the group least likely to have gambled privately, at an unlicensed establishment, or at a store, bar, restaurant, truck stop, or similar location.

While older adults are less likely than younger adults to have ever gambled or to have gambled in the past year, these individuals are just as likely—if not more likely—to gamble weekly. As Table 1 shows, 12 percent of adults ages 18 to 29 and 16 percent of adults ages 30 to 49 acknowledged gambling weekly; in contrast, 21 percent of adults ages 50 to 64 and 19 percent of adults ages 65 and over gamble weekly on one or more activities.

While gender and age are strong predictors of gambling, ethnicity also plays a role. Table 1 shows that lifetime and past-year gambling participation rates are significantly higher for whites than for other racial and ethnic groups in the United States. Meanwhile, weekly gambling participation is highest among African Americans. Still, there are substantial differences in the proportions of men and women in these ethnic groups who gamble: while 29 percent of black men and 21 percent of white men gamble weekly, only 17 percent of black women and 11 percent of white women gamble this frequently.

When it comes to participation in particular types of gambling, Table 2 shows that adults from all ethnic groups are equally likely to have gambled in the past year on the lottery, at a casino, or on a horse or dog race. However, white adults are substantially more likely than adults from other ethnic groups to have gambled in the past year on a charitable event, at a store, bar, or restaurant that offered only one gambling activity (usually video poker or some other type of gaming machine), at an unlicensed establishment, or at a tribal gaming operation. Nonwhite adults are more likely than whites to have gambled in the past year on bingo. Black adults are the least likely to have gambled in the past year on private types of wagering, such as card games in someone's home or on games of personal skill.

Attitudes Toward Gambling

Although gambling participation has increased since 1975, attitudes toward gambling have not changed dramatically in the United States. Most Americans hold complex and ambivalent rather than simple pro or anti attitudes about the effects of gambling on society. A Gallup survey in 1999 found that 29 percent of adults felt that gambling is immoral, compared with 27 percent in 1996 and 32 percent in 1992. The same survey found that only 22 percent of adults favored further expansion of legal gambling, while 47 percent favored the status quo and 29 percent wanted legal gambling opportunities reduced or banned outright. The reason for this general disinclination for the expansion of gambling was evidently that, while 67 percent of adults felt that casinos generally help a community's economy, 56 percent believed that casinos damage everyday family and community life.

As with gambling participation, age is a strong demographic predictor of attitudes toward gambling. On a five-point scale from very good to very bad, only 25 percent of eighteen- to twenty-nine-year-olds consider the overall effects of legalized gambling on society to be bad or very bad, a percentage that rises steadily by age group, reaching 56 percent among those sixty-five and older. There are no significant differences in this attitude by income or ethnicity, and only slight differences by sex and education, with males and those with less than a high school education tending to be slightly more positive about gambling's social effects.

While attitudes toward gambling remain complex, the reasons why people gamble have changed in the United States since 1975. The percentage of people who said they gambled in order to win money increased by one-half between 1975 and 1998, from 44 to 66 percent. In contrast, the percentage who said they gambled for excitement or challenge decreased by almost one-third, from 70 to 49 percent. The 1998 numbers tell a similar story to those of a 1993 Roper survey, which found that 75 percent of casino patrons said the primary reason they visit casinos is to win "a really large amount of money," while only 57 percent said that entertainment and recreation were important reasons they visit casinos. Americans in the 1990s and the new millennium appear to gamble less for the sheer joy of it and more as though it were a non-salaried second job, like day-trading or selling real estate. While people are now more likely to gamble in order to win money, the fact remains that most people who gamble, and especially those who gamble regularly, are most likely to lose money over the long run.

Reasons for gambling, like participation, vary by gender, age, and ethnicity. For example, men are more likely than women, and young adults (those ages eighteen to twenty-nine) are more likely than older adults, to say that they gamble for excitement. Young adults are also much more likely than adults ages sixty-five and older to say that winning money is an important reason to gamble. Among different racial and ethnic groups, Hispanics are more likely than blacks to say that they gamble in order to socialize, while blacks are more likely than whites or Hispanics to say that they gamble in order to win money. There are also ethnic differences in the reasons that nongamblers give for *not* gambling: only 29 percent of Hispanic nongamblers, versus 49 percent of black nongamblers and 58 percent of white nongamblers, refrained from gambling for moral reasons. Meanwhile, 72 percent of black nongamblers and 67 percent of white nongamblers—but only 54 percent of Hispanic nongamblers—refrained for financial reasons. These data suggest that Hispanics tend to approach gambling more as a social activity, and blacks more as a financial proposition.

Where Is Legal Gambling Headed?

It is difficult to forecast the evolution of legal gambling in America through the first decades of the twenty-first century. There are several trends that will influence this evolution, occasionally in opposite directions, including heightened participation of the middle class in legal forms of gambling, the spread of gambling to nongambling settings, and the looming impacts of gambling on the Internet. Other trends that may influence the evolution of legal gambling in the United States will be the continued availability of different types of gambling and concomitant changes in participation as people balance their gambling with other pursuits that they consider important.

Beyond the expansion in the availability of casinos and lotteries, the most notable change in Americans' access to gambling in the last two decades has been the shift in the availability of gambling from gambling-specific venues to a much wider range of social settings. Many forms of gambling, but especially electronic gaming devices (EGDs), are now available in bars, restaurants, hotels, social clubs, grocery and convenience stores, and even Laundromats—places where gambling was never previously available. Many of these operations have, in effect, become mini-casinos and sometimes are promoted as such.

While the consequences of this diffusion of gambling throughout society have yet to be adequately examined, convenience gambling was roundly condemned in the recent final report of the [1999] National Gambling Impact Study Commission. Certainly, the widespread appeal of EGDs to women and middle-class gamblers suggests that gambling participation rates will continue to increase, particularly in states where this type of gambling is introduced.

In contrast, the results of recent replication studies in several regions of the United States suggest that gambling participation may be declining. All of these data are drawn from telephone surveys with randomly selected respondents in the adult population, and all used similarly structured questionnaires that included questions about lifetime, past-year, and weekly gambling on a range of activities. Figure 1 presents information about the magnitude of changes in the proportion of respondents in each of five jurisdictions who have never gambled, who have gambled in the past year but not weekly, and who gamble weekly. These changes are presented in terms of magnitude rather than as changes in percentages in order to compare "apples with apples." The results are arrayed accord-

Changes in Gambling Participation Across Selected U.S. Jurisdictions

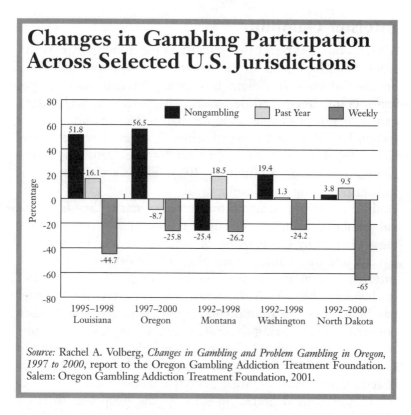

Source: Rachel A. Volberg, *Changes in Gambling and Problem Gambling in Oregon, 1997 to 2000*, report to the Oregon Gambling Addiction Treatment Foundation. Salem: Oregon Gambling Addiction Treatment Foundation, 2001.

ing to the interval between the baseline and the replication survey in each state.

The figure above shows that the proportion of respondents who were nongamblers increased in four of the five states under consideration. Similarly, the proportion of respondents who had gambled in the past year but did not gamble on a weekly basis increased in four of the five states. The clearest pattern in these data is that the proportion of respondents who gamble weekly or more often on one or more types of gambling decreased substantially in all five jurisdictions. While the decline was greatest in North Dakota between 1992 and 2000 and smallest in Washington State between 1992 and 1998, the declines in all of these jurisdictions were statistically significant. These data suggest that gambling participation rates may decline over time as people experiment with different activities and then stabilize their involvement to balance it with other important parts of their lives, including work and family commitments.

Internet Gambling

A final potential trend that will affect gambling participation is the looming impact of the Internet. Commercial gambling on the Internet, including blackjack, slot machines, bingo, keno, craps, horse and dog races, sports events, and lottery games, is now available on more than one thousand websites owned by 250 to 300 parent businesses or government agencies. Global consumer spending on Internet gambling is expected to reach $6.3 billion by 2003. There are a number of factors powering the development of Internet gambling, including consumer demand, the arrival of name brands, internal gambling industry pressures, the consumer price advantages created by the location of e-gambling businesses in tax havens, and the enabling technology of the Internet itself. The Internet has the potential to be the strongest growth market for legal gambling over the next ten to twenty years. Internet gambling sites are multiplying rapidly, and more and more countries are legalizing these activities and bringing them under regulatory control. Examples include not only remote Caribbean and Mediterranean islands, but also major industrialized nations, such as Great Britain and Australia.

In the United States, in spite of the proposed Internet Gambling Prohibition Act, a recent conviction of an off-shore sports book operator, and the National Gambling Impact Study Commission's recommendation that Congress criminalize Internet gambling, market forces are overwhelming legislative and judicial efforts to halt the migration of gamblers to cyberspace. Unsure of its legality and concerned for their licenses, established gambling suppliers in the United States have hesitated to embrace Internet gambling. Consumers have been less discriminating—a recent study in Oregon found that participation in all types of gambling, including casino and lottery games, had declined or remained stable between 1997 and 2000 with one exception: although starting from an extremely low base rate in 1997, lifetime Internet gambling participation increased by 260 percent and past-year Internet gambling grew by 600 percent.

It may be possible to discourage Americans from gambling on the Internet through legislation aimed at gambling operators as well as at the financial institutions that mediate payments between operators and customers. However, it is unlikely that criminalization will eradicate Internet gambling. Furthermore, given the interest of many state and tribal governments as well as private operators in developing Internet gambling sites, it may be that this "Pandora's box" is already open.

CHAPTER

2

EXAMINING POP CULTURE

Las Vegas: America's Gamble in the Desert

Las Vegas Reshapes American Life

John M. Findlay

In 1931, Nevada became the first state to legalize gambling after two decades of nationwide prohibition. It wasn't until the mid-1950s, however, that the newly developed casino resorts on the Las Vegas Strip—the city's neon-drenched boulevard of hotels and round-the-clock gambling—began to attract millions of Americans eager to lose themselves, and often their money, in the futuristic fantasy world of Las Vegas.

In the following excerpt from his book *People of Chance: Gambling in American Society from Jamestown to Las Vegas*, John M. Findlay examines the rise of the Las Vegas Strip and contends that it was highly influential in the cultural reshaping of mid–twentieth-century America. A stay on the Strip redefined leisure for middle-class Americans as an exciting, mass-marketed consumer activity and became the prototype for vacations in the United States. The Strip resorts offered gamblers the opportunity to challenge the stifling conformity of the Cold War era in an atmosphere of anything goes. In Findlay's view, the Strip was a Disneyland for adults, far removed from mainstream America, where risk and autonomy had been all but eradicated from daily life. The author is a professor of American history at the University of Washington in Seattle.

■

John M. Findlay, *People of Chance: Gambling in American Society from Jamestown to Las Vegas*. New York: Oxford University Press, 1986. Copyright © 1986 by John M. Findlay. Reproduced by permission of the publisher.

ON THE EVENING OF APRIL 4, 1955, THE OWNERS of the Last Frontier Hotel turned their backs on the bygone era of old West nostalgia and opened their doors to the age of the future. As they closed up the casino of the original hotel, they directed patrons around the corner and up the Strip to the entrance of a recently completed addition called the New Frontier. Like the updated name, the new annex could hardly have expressed better the mood of Americans in midcentury Las Vegas. Instead of the old West style that had prevailed at the Last Frontier, opening-night crowds now encountered modern luxuries couched in the most futuristic designs in the resort city. A switch in hotel slogans, from "The Old West in Modern Splendor" to "Out of this World," summarized the changed outlook and announced the space-age decor. . . .

The Futuristic "Strip"

The conversion from Last Frontier to New Frontier, from small, woodsy, auto court to large, garish, resort hotel, exemplified the dramatic changes that Las Vegas underwent after World War II. By the mid-1950s the population of the city proper had reached 50,000, while close to 100,000 people resided in the metropolitan area of Clark County. Eight million tourists spent $160 million in Las Vegas during 1956, demonstrating its nationwide popularity and providing the economic underpinnings so essential to its runaway growth. The dynamism of rapid expansion sprang not from Glitter Gulch [original gambling center in downtown Las Vegas], where decorators still enshrined the old West, but from the Strip [neon-lit boulevard of casino-resorts outside of downtown Las Vegas], which stretched toward the future because it led to Los Angeles. . . .

The futuristic Strip captured the imaginations of Americans. The resort city presented to visitors, in packages of three days and two nights, the attitudes and leisure of tomorrow. To a nation preoccupied with affluence and technology, roadtown Las Vegas appeared as a city designed for comfort and convenience. To a generation less burdened with doubts about gaming, Las Vegas offered a permissive atmosphere in which people freely took chances without seeming to suffer injury. To a people increasingly comfortable with the processes and commodities of large-scale consumer and service industries, Las Vegas proffered mass-produced, mass-merchandised vacations at prices great numbers of Americans could afford. The culture of the coming decades appeared to be on preview today for tourists in southern Nevada.

The postwar rise of the desert resort was in a sense a tale of two futuristic cities, for the development of the Las Vegas Strip amounted to little more than another subdivision of metropolitan Los Angeles. Increasingly during the middle decades of the century, observers recognized the close bond between the two urban areas. The legendary sleuth Lew Archer deduced the connection as he observed midday traffic in Las Vegas: "It came from every state in the Union, but most of the license plates belonged to Southern California. This carney town was actually Los Angeles's most farflung suburb.". . .

In fact, throughout the postwar years, Southern Californians amounted to between three-fifths and three-fourths of all visitors to Las Vegas. The resort catered successfully to the preferences of Angelenos and consolidated their novel values and styles of living.

Southern Nevada served as a backyard to which Angelenos retired for recreation. There they found the kinds of leisure that resembled in form and substance the amusements that Los Angeles itself had cultivated extensively. In the production of movies and television shows, and in the utilization of such theme amusement parks as Disneyland which had spun off from the entertainment industry, Southern Californians developed particularly commercial types of leisure that revolved in part around fantasy, that is, around the participant's willing suspension of disbelief. Recreation in Las Vegas not only borrowed the very personalities, economies, and architecture of leisure from Los Angeles; in gambling it also relied on the same element of fantasy among players. In both places the suspension of disbelief in play activities made all things seem possible. . . .

Pioneering Leisure

As a center of changes in the nature of recreation, the gambling capital had a disproportionately large role in transmitting new styles to the rest of the country. Americans could test novel forms of leisure more easily than they could experiment with other aspects of futuristic culture. Easterners may have been too tied to the central city to embrace suburban living, too attached to subways or elevated trains to accept automobility, or too reliant on traditional modes of production to participate in postindustrial economic activities. Outside of working life, however, they could be exposed to new cultural trends more readily. At home they could see the movies and television shows that Hollywood produced, and on vacations they could try out Californian styles of play. Trips to Disneyland, and later to Disney World, became a common experience for young Americans, and gambling vacations in southern Nevada permitted adults as well to taste for themselves the futuristic ways of life taking shape in Southern California.

The desert resort offered a combination of pleasures that could be experienced in such an easy and single-minded fashion nowhere else in the United States. Las Vegas operators toiled to provide a wide variety of pastimes for visitors. Each Strip hotel featured a number of bars or cocktail lounges, different restaurants and coffee shops, and at least one dinner-theater. Golf courses, swimming pools, tennis courts, riding stables, and still more athletic facilities were laid out on hotel grounds for guests. Resort hotels competed among themselves to attract the finest, most popular entertainers, often paying astronomical salaries even while charging minimal admission. Moreover, they all obtained not just one major show for the dinner-theater, but also a variety of lesser acts for other lounges and auditoriums in the different resort complexes along the Los Angeles highway. Nonetheless, the distinguishing feature of Las Vegas, the activity that set the town apart from other American resorts in substance rather than degree only, the financial centerpiece of the city, was casino gambling. Although other attractions gained popularity among tourists, betting prevailed as the major drawing card in southern Nevada. Gambling played a central role in the vision of tomorrow that Las Vegas projected.

Casino gaming was probably neither more nor less appealing to postwar Americans than it had been to other peoples in other times, for gambling has held a timeless interest around the world. From both the experience of casino betting and the setting of Las Vegas Strip hotels, however, Americans derived a significance that reflected the orientations of their society in the 1940s and 1950s. . . .

The Recreation Revolution

While Las Vegas vacations were hardly typical moments in the lives of postwar Americans, they nonetheless expressed broad social trends; the basic pattern of culture *was* appreciably affected. Tourists in southern Nevada perhaps left behind their hometown existences and indulged in fantasy, but they neither escaped reality nor denied the rigors of work and the tensions of Cold War society. Rather, they tested a vision of the years to come. As an offshoot of Los Angeles and as the nation's gambling capital, Las Vegas figured prominently in the cultural reshaping of the United States. More than a "set of parentheses" in people's lives, the city, and the Las Vegas Strip in particular, portended what the future held in store for Americans of the postwar period. The tremendous attention paid to the desert resort, the huge number of visitors, and the enormous sums of money spent there all certified that, in its own completely secular way, Las Vegas stood "as a city upon a hill" for Cold War Americans, demonstrating the direction and meaning of cultural change. Tom Wolfe, ace reporter of contemporary styles, concluded in 1965 that the gambling capital represented "the super-hyper-version of a whole new way of life."

Las Vegas proved particularly instructive about the implications of a veritable revolution in recreation in the United States. After decades of a gradual shift in the balance between work and play, Americans became increasingly preoccupied with the consumption of leisure after World War II. The unforeseen affluence, the relaxation of wartime restraints on travel and purchasing, and essential technological advances all compelled Americans first to recognize leisure clearly as a division of their lives' time, and then to devote more attention to spending that time in a satisfying manner. The experiences of depression and war doubtless helped to lay the groundwork for these changes. The forced idleness of the unemployed and underemployed during the 1930s and of servicemen during the Second World War taught people how to find and structure amusement, and the "moral lapse" that presumably follows upon the heels of war prepared the nation to accept more diverse modes of recreation.

In the years around midcentury Americans were persuaded that the amount of leisure was growing and would continue to grow in the future. Whether they truly had more free time remains unclear, and the extent of their off-hours never matched predictions of an increasingly work-free society. Nonetheless, that Americans thought they had more time for play, and that social scientists devoted more attention to recreation, certainly evinced the growing significance of leisure in the United States. The importance of time devoted to leisure increasingly gained ground on the importance of the working week. Such a transformation signified the emergence of a postindustrializing society. . . .

More laborers interrupted the working day with breaks, more businessmen took extended lunches, and more people attended conventions, often in resort cities like Las Vegas, where job-related activities came to be intermixed with play. David Riesman observed that, "reminiscent in some ways of the pre-industrial age," the strands of work and leisure became "increasingly indistinct" and more intertwined as the boundaries between the worlds of "application" and diversion began to disappear. The meaning of leisure was consequently redefined. As Americans incorporated forms of leisure into their working hours, they also began to work harder at play. It quickly became clear that leisure would no longer be so leisurely any more. . . .

Extreme "Play"

In intensity and pace, gambling holidays in Las Vegas became the prototype for vacations in the postindustrializing United States. Growing participation in organized athletics and outdoor life, as well as heightened attendance at amusement parks, illustrated how Americans worked harder at recreation, but in Nevada gambling sprees the changes in the nature of play reached new extremes. Seemingly unconcerned that casinos had arranged vacation activities so as to require the minimum of effort, tourists consumed leisure as earnestly as they could, particularly in the gambling halls where players slaved away at games as if there were no tomorrow and no yesterday. With no clocks provided by the management, gamblers lost all track of time in casinos. Moreover, encouraged by an atmosphere of fantasy and by casinos' policy of converting currency to plastic chips, vacationers also lost track of the customary value of money. It was as if players' psychological moorings to the industrial culture of America, their senses of time and money, had unraveled. John Pastier, an architectural historian, suggested that, without keeping conventional track of time or money, gamblers in Las Vegas could "experience the present moments as intensely as the inhabitants of a preindustrial society."

Perhaps the diminished senses of time and money that enabled tourists in Las Vegas to experience play so intensely did not resemble preindustrial conditions so much as they characterized the nature of leisure in postindustrial society, especially as it emerged in Southern California and southern Nevada. Gambling vacations encompassed the most far-reaching changes in the relationship between work and play. As the cutting edge of the revolution in recreation, Las Vegas offered tourists not a place to get away from it all but rather a sleepless and timeless atmosphere of excitement, tension, and pressure. There visitors consumed leisure time in a most unleisurely manner, spending themselves and their money heatedly at a variety of diversions and places. All activities revolved around casino betting, which epitomized frantic play in the resort city.

Gambling Is Character-Defining

Casino betting appealed to postwar society not only because it suited the new balance between work and leisure but also because it helped people develop a stronger sense of self. Finding individuality threatened by the rising economic culture of mass production, average Americans turned more and more to consumption of goods, services, and leisure time as a mode of personal expression. Observers noticed the trend relatively early in Los Angeles, where residents commonly defined individuality in terms of such possessions as cars and homes. As pioneers of the new age, Southern Californians seized very quickly the opportunity to pursue individuality less through economic endeavors and more through cultural channels. Consumption of material goods constituted one source of identity and individuality, but Angelenos also achieved personal fulfillment as accomplished consumers of leisure. They and other Americans invested play with a greater importance, as indicated by the serious, worklike attitude they brought to it. They also sought out those activities, like casino gambling, that promised to demonstrate most clearly where they stood as individuals in the mass society of the mid-twentieth-century.

Contemporary social scientists who analyzed gambling generally agreed that the games were well suited to the process of defining personal identity. In an era when individuality and economic risk seemed to dwindle in importance next to the stress on collective security, betting made up an arena of endeavor where individuality continued to flourish, where chance could still be enjoyed at an intensely personal level. Erving Goffman explained that gambling provided people with an opportunity to "achieve character," to develop personal reputation. In a society where risk had been "all but arranged out of everyday life," people could still prove themselves through play in public casinos. Character established at gaming tables was regarded as an accurate measure of one's mettle because it was attained in the face of hazards undertaken "without obligation." Character came to be enhanced not so much by winning or losing, but by maintaining "full self control when the chips are down." Reputation depended first upon whether a person gambled at all, whether he would expose himself to unnecessary risks, and second upon how, not how successfully, he played the game. Character came to be gambled, then, along with money. Casino betting enabled people as consumers of leisure time to define for themselves a stronger sense of reputation.

The atmosphere inside casinos located along the Los Angeles highway facilitated the pursuit of individuality and character that betting entailed. Strip casinos offered patrons a blend of sociability and autonomy that proved ideal for wagering character. Unlike downtown gambling halls, which relied more on solitary games like the slot machines, keno, and bingo, roadtown resorts emphasized more social games such as craps, roulette, and twenty-one, where players gathered around tables. These games provided an audience in front of which individual bettors had to establish reputation. The presence of other players increased the psychological stakes by making the wager of character a public event.

Mass Autonomy

Yet few players actually paid much attention to each other. From all walks of life and from all corners of the globe, people crowded into downtown and Strip casinos largely unaware of one another. The anonymous throngs induced a sense of self-reliance. Bettors almost inevitably played Las Vegas as individuals, and that helped them perceive more directly the character they were establishing. The anonymity and permissiveness of casinos, and the solitude inherent in gambling, lent to players a feeling of autonomy that once again served to heighten individuality in an age of the "lonely crowd.". . .

In gambling, Las Vegas tourists could challenge the stifling conformity and affluence of the Cold War era and resist the sense of aimlessness that accompanied postwar change. Although the risks undertaken were generally small and safe, gamblers derived disproportionately strong senses of personal satisfaction and identity from betting, senses that helped them to understand and to accept where they stood as individuals in the fluctuating culture of the United States. The experience appealed especially to Californians and other Westerners, whose restless and atomistic society was predicated on private confrontations with chance and change.

That people developed a sense of individuality while gambling in Las Vegas proved paradoxical. Americans rushed en masse to southern Nevada and acquired a greater sense of self amidst huge crowds at supermarkets of gambling. Although betting was experienced at an intensely personal level, it was undertaken by large numbers thronging together at gaming tables. Casinos manufactured and marketed their product as if by assembly line processes with virtually no regard for the individuality of consumers. . . .

The Primacy of Money

Moreover, although bettors hoped to develop senses of themselves that would set them apart from the crowd, gaming tended to reduce everything and everybody to a single common denominator—money. The sound, the feel, and the appearance of money pervaded each gaming table and each casino and hotel interior, from downtown clubs that displayed tens of thousands of dollars in cash in their lobbies, to roadtown hotels decked out in the most luxurious furnishings. Because the common denominator of money seemed to underlay all aspects of the desert resort, William Saroyan concluded that Las Vegas had developed a single-mindedness about it. "Some place in the richest nation in the world," he mused, "there has to be a city with no other excuse for being than money." But money was the means as well as the end in Las Vegas, the medium as well as the message. It lent significance to games that would otherwise have been empty, even though from the outset players understood the probable outcome of the action. In other words, satisfaction, excitement, and even reputation came from gambling with money, and with character, not necessarily from winning or losing. Beyond the actual games, money served as a medium of communicaton, of advertisement, of architecture in Las Vegas; it prevailed everywhere in one form or another.

The primacy of money in Las Vegas proved to be as paradoxical as the mass achieving of individuality in gaming. On the one hand money translated into luxury beyond the means of the average citizen. From the deep-pile carpets to the space-age chandeliers, wealth permeated resort hotels on the Strip. Publicists dramatized the lives of the rich and famous, and at every turn patrons might be reminded that casino gambling had traditionally been the exclusive province of upper classes around the world.

Middle-Class Appeal

On the other hand, however, gambling vacations in Las Vegas were generally tailored to the great American middle class, because there lay the profits for the resort industry of the mid-twentieth century. Prices in the desert city remained mostly moderate and the atmosphere remained largely informal. Contemporary observers stressed the egalitarian and unexclusive nature of Nevada gambling. Comparing Las Vegas to European gaming resorts, English playwright Noel Coward found crowds in Las Vegas composed of "the most ordinary people." The urban resort catered to the middle strata of society, and in this way more than any other demonstrated that it was an achievement of mid-twentieth-century American civilization. As a resort for the masses, it broke with the long tradition of gambling spas for the rich, and the contrasts appeared everywhere. Whereas aristocratic Monte Carlo in 1879 had celebrated the completion of an opera house and theater and the debut of the exclusive *salle privée* with a poetry reading by Sarah Bernhardt, "Bugsy" Siegel's Flamingo Hotel opened in the late 1940s with the comedy team of Abbott and Costello.

Employing a facade of luxury and wealth, hotels and casinos on the Strip appealed as successfully to the middle classes as the downtown clubs adhering to the more common motif of the old West. Entrepreneurs in Las Vegas quickly realized that in the gambling business the most money would be made from high volume, so they mass-produced and mass-marketed gambling vacations for the wide American public. The astounding prosperity of the resort city was predicated not on a few wealthy "high-rollers," nor on serious gamblers who might work the casinos skillfully, but on millions of small-scale bettors whose average length of stay spanned three days and two nights. These tourists lost just enough money to provide sizable profits for the casino industry, but never enough to deter them from return visits to Las Vegas. Such consumers were the raw material for the gambling industry which grew up in southern Nevada, an industry that mass-merchandised the transitory leisure experience of gambling in an unprecedented environment.

When Gangsters Ran Las Vegas Casinos

David Spanier

For most of its history as America's gambling capital, Las Vegas has played the role of Sin City in popular culture, a place where adults could come to indulge in activities forbidden in the rest of the country. The city's dangerous, transgressive image has been undermined in recent years by the spread of legalized gambling outside of Nevada and by the corporate repackaging of Las Vegas as a family-friendly destination during the 1990s. But as David Spanier maintains in the following excerpt from his book *Welcome to the Pleasuredome: Inside Las Vegas*, part of Las Vegas's appeal to tourists has rested on its reputation as a city of vice founded by notorious organized crime figures. As the author describes, mobsters opened the first casino resorts on the Las Vegas Strip and held sway over the city until tough new licensing procedures for running the casinos brought their reign to an end in the early 1980s. Spanier, who died in 2000, was a gambling enthusiast and authored several other books on the subject, including *Easy Money: Inside the Gambler's Mind* and *Total Poker*.

WHERE DID THE MAFIA GO? LAS VEGAS IS SUP-posed to be a mob town. Stories of Mafia involvement, of skimming and fraud, of gangster rivalry, of torture and mur-

■

der, are part of the stock in trade of the place. Yet nowadays, everyone, from the regulatory authorities and casino managers right down the line, protests that Las Vegas is clear of the Mafia. In the '90s, they claim, Las Vegas . . . entered a new era, squeaky clean. Can it really be true that the wise guys have been driven out of town? Does human nature, in this case human greed, ever change?

Screening Out the Mafia

Some things do change. Foremost among which is the licensing procedure for running a casino. In the old days,—'Hard times make hard people,' as people like Moe Dalitz [Midwest mobster who moved to Las Vegas in the 1950s] liked to say—anyone could get into the business, because out there, in the West, you didn't ask a man a whole bunch of questions. Now it is very, very tough. The process is lengthy and thorough and almost unforgivably intrusive into applicants' private lives. The process of investigation, in fact, is said to be more rigorous than security clearance for politically sensitive posts in Washington. Everything the investigators can uncover in an applicant's past—bank statements, income tax returns, private correspondence, down to the smallest detail, comes under scrutiny. No scrap of paper is too insignificant to attract official attention, even—to cite a recent instance—an applicant's wife's Christmas card list. One man who was subjected to this kind of inquisition recently, himself the author of a standard text on casino management, told me that his interrogation, which lasted nearly six months, was the worst and most humiliating experience of his life.

The licensing authorities' motivation is clear and simple. It is to eliminate applicants who have had any kind of association with the Mafia, however light or indirect it might have been. A worthy aim, and a necessary one given Las Vegas' past.

It was the [Estes] Kefauver [former U.S. senator from Tennessee] hearings of 1950–51 which first focused national attention on organized crime. Kefauver and his team spent only a couple of days in Vegas, a place which the Senator obviously disliked on principle before he ever got there. Kefauver was widely thought to be furthering his presidential ambitions by the root and branch condemnation of illicit gambling in his report. But that didn't diminish the impact it had. 'Gambling profits are the principle support of big-time racketeering and gangsterism', he reported.

The bad reputation of Las Vegas was further highlighted by the lurid exposure of mob operations reported in *The Green Felt Jungle* by Ovid Demaris and Ed Reid, which had a major impact on public opinion in Nevada, and beyond. The book named all the bad guys, listing in gruesome detail their criminal activities in the leading casinos—at that time, around 1963, there were eleven casino-hotels on the Strip, each one of them, so it seemed, more corrupt than the next.

The current licensing system was introduced by a reforming State Governor, Grant Sawyer, in 1959–67, and was elaborated under his successors. Sawyer's instructions to his team were: 'Get tough and stay tough'. In those days, recalls Sawyer (now a partner in a law firm), the corruption in the industry was rank. There was widespread alarm in Nevada that as things stood the Federal Government, in the person of Attorney-General Robert Kennedy [who served under his brother, then-president John F. Kennedy from 1961–63], intended to introduce legislation to prohibit states' gambling altogether. This would have done more than clean up Nevada, it would have wrecked the state's economy. Sawyer campaigned to bring the industry under state control and won election somewhat against the odds. But while the new licensing rules might screen new applicants very effectively, the authorities couldn't get rid of the good ol' boys like Moe Dalitz, who were already in the woodwork. . . .

Banking on Its Dangerous Image

Yet in a funny way, Las Vegas' reputation as a haven for the mob has been part of its attraction, its glamour. Nevada's dangerous image, as a recent chairman of the Gaming Commission, John O'Reilly, observed, has probably attracted tourism. When people gamble—particularly in American society, where everyone has been raised to believe in thrift and hard work—they want to feel an edge of excitement, of transgression, of living on the edge. I have heard local people say, only half in jest, that day-to-day life in town was a lot safer when the mob was in charge—that the wise guys ran things their way and kept the muggers and sneak thieves off the streets. Nowadays, you would think twice before walking into an un-lit car park. In the classless equality of the gaming tables, the Mafia-types were regarded as dudes of the game.

It is still hard to believe, whatever officials may claim, that the Mafia has left town and lost its influence. After all, where is it *not* found in American city life? Anyone browsing in the Gambler's Book Club [a Las Vegas bookstore], that treasure trove of gaming lore, will find a whole shelf of books detailing Mafia connections with gambling, including not one, but two, full length biographies of John Gotti, the man reputed to be the boss of organised crime in New York City. Such figures are written up in the media like movie stars. The shiny image of the Mafia, the way its members are fêted and looked up to in restaurants and night clubs and on the showbiz fringe was brilliantly depicted in Martin Scorsese's movie *GoodFellas* (1990). What seems to be true in Las Vegas is that the Mafia—or Cosa Nostra as its members refer to their fraternity—is no longer *directly* involved in running gambling. Beyond the new licensing procedures, the change from personal to corporate ownership of most of the major casinos has created a completely different business structure. The Mafia has been driven to the fringes of the gambling business, first of all at street level in drug trafficking. Las Vegas is notorious as a lucrative outlet for the drug gangs operating in Los Angeles. Indeed it has the second highest drugs abuse record of any place in the United States, obviously a reflection on the transient population.

Secondly, there is probably a mob connection with prostitution in Vegas. All the services masquerading under entertainment, listed in the Yellow Pages, which send exotic dancers and escorts direct to the caller's hotel room, imply a degree of pimping or behind the scenes organisation, even though the licensed brothels [prostitution is legal in parts of Nevada] themselves seem to be private enterprises. And thirdly, it has been suggested that the Mafia or their associates may have tried to penetrate middle management, at some weak points, after licensing and ownership regulations were tightened up. There are going to be some dishonest people in any kind of business, and especially in a business with a gigantic cash flow like casino gambling. But to suggest that the Mafia might have succeeded in planting contacts here and there—like spies engaged in espionage in a foreign country—shows how far Vegas has changed from the days when major casinos were seen, literally, as 'Our Thing', Cosa Nostra.

Exploring the Chain of Corruption

The most vivid account of the rise and fall of organised crime in Las Vegas that I have seen, was a documentary called 'Mob on the Run' by a television reporter named Ned Day. It was made for a programme called *Eyewitness News* on the local station KLAS TV, screened in the spring of 1987. Not long after his programme was shown, Ned Day—still in his early 40s—drowned while on vacation in Hawaii. Was Ned Day's untimely death, after his exposé of organised crime on a popular TV programme, an act of petty vengeance, to be taken as a warning to prying journalists? Apparently not. According to the evidence, there was no suspicion of foul play. (The Mafia do not operate outside their own territory, so one is assured.) What Day's programme did was to present, *visually*, the progress of Chicago's operations in Las Vegas, in context. It conveyed, in a matter of fact but dramatic way, the chain of corruption and how it all worked.

Day began with [gangsters] Meyer Lansky and Benjamin "Bugsy" Siegel coming into town in 1941, 'our founding fathers'. A shifty, brutal-looking pair; but nothing compared with former mob killer turned informant, 'Jimmy the Weasel' Fratianno, who resentfully explained to camera how the Jews among these early gangsters got so big at the expense of the Italians. 'The Jews showed money. They had money. You give an Italian a million dollars he puts it under the cellar . . . That's where the Italians made a mistake. They shoulda done it themselves.' The Mafia preferred to work through surrogates, partners like Bugsy Siegel, or front men like Wilbur Clark, vague as a will o' the wisp about business matters, at the Desert Inn.

Behind every success story, there is usually one good idea. The real trick of the mob, in getting hidden control of casinos, lay in using its bankroll for investment. (In the late '50s and '60s banks and insurance companies did not dream of investing in the casino business: this was long before junk bonds). The jackpot in terms of cash was the Teamsters' Central States Pension Fund in Chicago. The Chicago crime family, led by Sam Giancana from 1956 to the late 1960s, (later shot in the basement of his Chicago home), achieved extraordinary influence in controlling this fund. Their link man was Allen Dorfman (son of an old Al Capone [1920s Chicago gangster] gunslinger), who built up a very close relationship with the Teamsters' leadership. Working hand in glove with corrupt officials, in particular one Roy Lee Williams, he was able to manipulate the Pension Fund's huge resources to obtain 'loans' for front men, to buy up or finance casinos in Vegas. The Fund became, in effect, a private bank for the Chicago syndicate.

In 1973 Allen Glick, a thirty-two-year-old businessman from San Diego, suddenly popped up. He bought up all the shares and became owner of the Stardust. How did a young man, with no money of his own and no experience of casinos, pick such a plum? Glick happened to go to college with the son of the mob boss of Milwaukee; the son recommended Glick to his father, who recommended him to Chicago—'and presto', reported William Roemer, the distinguished FBI agent, in his memoirs *Man Against the Mob*, 'this young kid with no background in gaming gets a $62.75m. loan from the Central States Pension Fund.' A few months later he got further loans totalling $30m.

The chain of corruption extended. Caesars, Circus Circus, the Aladdin, the Stardust, the Fremont, the Dunes, were all funded with the aid of Chicago mob money. As the casinos prospered, the 'points', or percentage shares of ownership, held by mob leaders grew ten or even a hundred-fold in value. It was Lansky's role, living in Miami, far away from the action, to keep track of everyone's interests: he had the financial acumen and, most important, was trusted by his partners in crime to keep the record straight, according to *Little Man*, a biography of Lansky by Robert Lacey.

A Cast of Villains from Chicago

The Mafia loved the casino business. Not only did it gush cash like an oil well—it also had glamour. From the earliest days there had been a mutual attraction between Hollywood and Vegas, with the razzmatazz of opening nights, flying visits by stars, gossip column tattle. Bugsy Siegel knew all the movie stars (and was himself a sort of star). Many came as guests to the Flamingo [casino opened by Siegel in 1947, the first major gambling operation on what became the Las Vegas Strip]. The showbiz connexion with Vegas, always close, was personified by Frank Sinatra [popular 1950s singer who performed in Las Vegas casinos], noblest Roman of them all, as Caesars Palace once put it. It was not all sparkly good times but from the mob's point of view the star names shimmering down from a hundred signs and billboards along the Strip were a guarantee of success.

The master-image in the cast of villains assembled by Ned Day in his TV report was Tony 'Big Tuna' Accardo. A former bodyguard of Al Capone, suspected as one of the gunmen in the St. Valentine's Day Massacre [on February 14, 1929, seven members of Chicago mobster Bugs Moran's gang were found murdered], he had been a long time consigliere of the Chicago family. Big Tuna was caught on camera, by the time of his trial a fierce, bent, old man, one leg half-twisted under him, shuttling rapidly forward like a crab. He grasped a walking stick, displaying on the handle the superb golden-scaled head of a fish, like the symbol of authority of a renaissance prince. His presence exuded evil and power.

Big Tuna's great coup was to consolidate Chicago's grip on Vegas to the virtual exclusion of all the other crime families. He secured this prize by an astute piece of diplomacy, in negotiating a division of spoils a year ahead of the opening of casino gambling in Atlantic City, New Jersey, in the summer of 1978. According to Roemer's account, at a meeting of 'the Commission', the ruling body of the national mob, Chicago advanced a proposition: 'You guys in the East take Atlantic City. Chicago will take Nevada.' At first the eastern mobsters protested. Joey Aiuppa, representing Accardo, who had coached him in his lines, told them: 'We will grandfather you guys in'—i.e. protect their interests for them. The argument made sense: the eastern mob families would be given the run of the Boardwalk in return for Chicago retaining undisputed sway on the Strip.

The Rise of Little Tony

Through the 1970s and most of the '80s, the Chicago mob's interests came under the control of one of the nastiest gangsters ever blown out of the windy city, a cold, cruel killer named Tony Spilotro. Short and stocky, nicknamed Tony the Ant or Little Tony because of his baby-faced look, he had arrived in America, uneducated and alone, at the age of fourteen. His vicious streak showed early on, in petty crime. He became a 'soldier', climbing up the organisation over the corpses of his victims. His brutality had commended him to a gangster named DeStefano, who dominated loan-sharking in Chicago: on one occasion DeStefano had hoisted a rival on a meat hook, to torture–murder him. When, in his turn, DeStefano was gunned down, Spilotro was the suspected killer. By that time he had risen to the lower levels of 'the Outfit', as the crime syndicate in Chicago (founder Al Capone) was known. In 1971 Little Tony was sent to Vegas as an enforcer, to ensure the cash funnelled from the mob casinos flowed back to the bosses in Chicago. He had a swaggering, ruthless style, at odds with his baby features, and a reputation which sent the chill of death into everyone he encountered. Even in his own milieu he was despised: 'this guy's an animal, a punk, with no class, no finesse,' one old mobster, Johnny Roselli, who worked as a coordinator in Las Vegas, described him. Since 1960 he had been arrested, questioned or listed as a suspect—but never convicted—in at least 25 mob-style killings. Many were marked by the same trademark: shots fired at close range into the eardrum, mouth and forehead from a small-calibre pistol fitted with a silencer, according to a series of articles in the Los Angeles *Times* by Michael J. Goodman.

Spilotro began by securing the lease (under his wife's name) of the jewellery-gift counter at Circus Circus. This was a valuable concession in itself, which could not be obtained without 'juice'. It so happened that the major owner of the casino at that time had borrowed nearly $20m. from the Chicago-based Teamsters' pension fund. The jewellery store became the centre of Spilotro's rapidly expanding operations, until he moved to the Sands, and then—after heavy pressure on its members by his partner, Frank 'Lefty' Rosenthal—the swanky Las Vegas Country Club. One of the Club's founders was none other than Moe Dalitz.

In the first three years after Spilotro's arrival, more Mafia-type murders occurred in Vegas than in the previous 25 years.

He soon overtook Rosenthal, who as a Jew could never be inducted into the highest levels of the Outfit. Under Spilotro's rule an enormous range of crimes, big and small, were perpetrated all over town. (He even organised burglaries at the homes of his neighbours—which refutes any fond idea that Vegas was a safer place under Mafia control.)

Skimming with 'Lefty'

In contrast with Tony the Ant, his old pal Frank 'Lefty' Rosenthal, whom he teamed up with in Vegas, was unthreatening. Operator of a sports book and reputedly the sharpest odds maker in the country, he had a long record of misdeeds (including a run-in with the law for fixing a college basket ball game in Carolina). Now he was working on the inside track, as a senior executive at the Stardust, though without ever obtaining a licence. When Spilotro came to town, Rosenthal's role was organiser and link-man, reporting directly to the mob bosses in Chicago. 'All the skimming, and believe me . . . they're skimming the shit out of these joints, is Lefty's responsibility', Roselli confided to hitman 'Jimmy the Weasel' Fratianno (in *The Last Mafioso* by Ovid Demaris). The partnership between Rosenthal and Spilotro—Mr Inside and Mr Outside—was the axle around which all Mafia activity in Vegas turned.

The mob's favourite method of making money out of casinos was by skimming. This means lifting money illicitly, either between the tables and the counting room or in the counting room before the daily tally is taken, explains William Roemer. Skimming can only be accomplished with the connivance of casino employees and by evading security cameras. According to Roemer, the money skimmed in Vegas was Chicago's number one source of income for more than two decades.

Probably the greatest coup which Rosenthal masterminded for the Chicago outfit was the skimming operation at the Stardust. Under his direction, the Stardust had been completely penetrated. A separate counting room was set up for the slots, with false scales for weighing the money. Thanks to this scam, the mob was skimming up to $40,000 a week in coins and another $40,000 in hundred dollar notes. A parallel scam was practised on the drop boxes from the tables. The FBI eventually broke the Stardust racket, thanks to a wire-tap of a 'business meeting' between gangsters of various families who had assembled in Kansas City. . . .

The popular image of Las Vegas' corruption was spread by fiction, films and TV drama. 'Look,' one of the leading characters remarks in the novel *Fools Die* by Mario Puzo, 'we can always handle trouble with the federal government with our lawyers and the courts; we have judges and we have politicians. One way or another we can fix things with the governor and the gambling control commissions. The deputy's office runs the town the way we want it. I can pick up the phone and get almost anybody run out of town. We are building an image of Vegas as an absolute safe place for gamblers.' This was overstated, no doubt, but as the stories of corruption over the years bore out, not so wide of the mark for that time. For three or four years Spilotro seemed 'untouchable'. . . .

The Downfall of the Outfit

Spilotro was finally arrested in Vegas in January 1983 and extradited to Chicago, where he was later released on bail. . . . The same fate overtook Little Tony that he had meted out to so many others. Indeed in Mafia terms, his elimination made perfect sense. His organisation had grown sloppy, he was beset by legal troubles and was suffering the embarrassment of front page exposure in the press. Worst of all—from the mob's point of view—there was a suspicion that he was holding back money creamed in Vegas, which should have gone straight to the Outfit. Word was that he was even challenging for the leadership. One fine morning in June 1986 Spilotro and his brother were seen driving off from his suburban home in Chicago as usual. Nine days later their bodies were accidently uncovered in a cornfield in Indiana (not far from convicted Chicago crime boss Joey Aiuppa's farm.) They had been done to death in characteristically brutal fashion, by blows and kicks. At the time of his death Spilotro was suspect in at least 25 murder cases.

The collapse of the Stardust skim, the subsequent gaoling [jailing] of the Mafia ringleaders and the downfall of Spilotro knocked the stuffing out of the Chicago operation in Vegas. According to various sources, as reported by the Las Vegas *Review-Journal*, the whole town had become so hot that the crime bosses in Chicago ordered a 'hands off policy'. . . .

Banking on a Storied Past

In 'Mob on the Run' Ned Day compared the Mafia to an octopus whose tentacles reached out into all sections of society. In the federal wire-taps which exposed widespread corruption at the Tropicana, for example, Harry Reid, the Gaming Commission chairman was given the nickname 'Mr Clean Face' and described by the wise guys as 'bought and paid for'. Reid, who went on to become a Senator for Nevada, defended himself against such slurs, claiming that a lot of names were tossed around. Likewise Bob Miller, then District Attorney, was named in the tapes as a friend of Allen Dorfman, the mob associate who had exploited the [Teamsters'] pension fund. 'Dorfman was a friend of my late father,' Miller protested. 'Can I choose his friends?' Miller was elected Lieutenant Governor in 1986 and Governor in 1990. But Governor Bob List, who had accepted complimentary services from the Stardust when serving as Attorney-General, including so it was alleged 'booze and broads' parties provided by Lefty, was not re-elected. Senator [Howard W.] Cannon whom Dorfman and Williams were caught on tape conspiring to bribe, failed to secure re-election, after twenty-four years in office. As people like Rosenthal liked to say, defending their murky past, licensed gambling in the silver state grew out of illegal gaming: in that sense, everyone was linked to it, like an archaeological pattern of lines etched into the land.

Ned Day's programme wound up with an optimistic view of Las Vegas. The community had been forced to face the evidence of wrong-doing. It couldn't claim that it was all got up by the press or the feds. The convictions set the stage for the State to take control, with licensing and investigation of new applicants. There was no public relations disaster. On the contrary, the fame of Las Vegas spread wider: 'Las Vegas is poised for a great leap forward into a new golden age of economic prosperity. But the price of the future is never to forget the past.'

The "New" Las Vegas Entices the Nation

Kurt Andersen

In the late 1960s, scandals involving organized crime's infiltration of casinos in Las Vegas left the lingering impression that the city was too seedy for its own good, and tourism suffered. To clean up the city's image and restore credibility to the gambling industry, large corporations invested heavily in the Las Vegas Strip throughout the 1970s, and by the late 1980s had begun building gigantic theme-resorts with activities for the whole family. Gambling—or "gaming" as industry executives renamed it—remained the city's main attraction but was marketed as a fun-filled recreational activity, not a pastime for social deviants.

In the following article written in 1994 for *Time* magazine, Kurt Andersen contends that the corporate repackaging of Las Vegas has had a significant impact on American popular culture. Not only is the city booming and attracting record numbers of tourists, but the rest of the country has become "Las Vegas–sized," adopting its high-tech spectacle, twenty-four-hour convenience, and most important, its embrace of legalized gambling. According to the author, Las Vegas has become the perfect reflection of American culture and values. Andersen is a former editor and columnist for both the *New Yorker* and *Time* magazines and is the author of the 1999 novel *Turn of the Century*.

■

Kurt Andersen, "Las Vegas: The New All-American City," *Time*, vol. 143, January 10, 1994, pp. 42–51. Copyright © 1994 by Time, Inc. Reproduced by permission.

HOW CAN A LARGE-SPIRITED AMERICAN NOT LIKE Las Vegas, or at least smile at the notion of it? On the other hand, how can any civilized person not loathe Las Vegas, or at least recoil at its relentlessness?

How can you not love and hate a city so crazily go-go that three different, colossally theme-park-like casino-hotels (the $375 million Luxor, Steve Wynn's $475 million Treasure Island and now the $1 billion MGM Grand, the largest hotel on earth and the venue last weekend for [singer] Barbra Streisand's multimillion-dollar return to live, paid performing) have opened on the Strip in just the past three months [late 1993]? How can you not love and hate a city so freakishly democratic that at a hotel called the Mirage, futuristic-looking infomercial star Susan Powter and a premodern Mennonite [conservative Protestants who generally shun the modern world] family can pass in a corridor, neither taking note of the other? How can you not love and hate a city where the $100,000 paintings for sale at an art gallery appended to Caesars Palace (Patron: "He's a genius." Gallery employee: "Yes, he's so creative." Patron: "It gives me goose bumps.") are the work of [actor] Anthony Quinn?

In no other peacetime locale are the metaphors and ironies so impossibly juicy, so ripe for the plucking. And there are always new crops of redolent, suggestive Vegas facts, of which any several—for instance: the Mirage has a *$500-a-pull* slot-machine salon; the lung-cancer death rate here is the second highest in the country; the suicide rate and cellular-phone usage are the highest—constitute a vivid, up-to-date sketch of the place.

But it used to be that while Las Vegas was unfailingly piquant and over the top, it was sui generis, its own highly peculiar self. Vegas in none of its various phases (ersatz Old West outpost in the 1930s and '40s, gangsters-meet-Hollywood high-life oasis in the '50s and '60s, uncool polyester dump in the '70s and early '80s) was really an accurate prism through which to regard the nation as a whole.

Now, however, as the city ricochets through its biggest boom since the Frank-and-Dino Rat Pack [nickname for entertainers Frank Sinatra, Dean Martin, Sammy Davis Jr., Peter Lawford, and Joey Bishop] days of the '50s and '60s—the tourist inflow has nearly doubled over the past decade, and the area remains among America's fastest growing—the hyper-eclectic 24-hour-a-day fantasy-themed party machine no longer seems so very exotic or extreme. High-tech spectacle, convenience, classlessness, loose money, a Nikes-and-T-shirt dress code: that's why immigrants flock to the U.S.; that's why some 20 million Americans (and 2 million foreigners) went to Vegas in 1992. "Las Vegas exists because it is a perfect reflection of America," says [casino entrepreneur] Steve Wynn, the city's most important and interesting resident. "You say 'Las Vegas' in Osaka or Johannesburg, anywhere in the world, and people smile, they understand. It represents all the things people in every city in America like. Here they can get it in one gulp." There is a Jorge Luis Borges story called *The Aleph* that describes the magical point where all places are seen from every angle. Las Vegas has become that place in America, less because of its own transformation in the past decade than because of the transformation of the nation. Las Vegas has become American-ized, and, even more, America has become Las Vegasized.

With its ecologically pious displays of white tigers and dolphins—and no topless show girls—the almost tasteful Mirage has profoundly enlarged and updated the notion of Vegas amusement since it opened in 1989. The general Las Vegas marketing spin today is that the city is fun for the whole family. It seems to be an effective p.r. line, but it's an idea that the owners of the new Luxor and MGM Grand may have taken too much to heart.

Inside the Luxor is a fake river and barges, plus several huge "participatory adventure" areas, an ersatz archaeological ride, as well as a two-story Sega virtual-reality video-game arcade. The joint has acres of casino space—but the slots and blackjack tables are, astoundingly, quite separate from and mostly concealed by the Disneyesque fun and games. The bells and whistles are more prominent and accessible than the casino itself, and are not merely a cute, quick way to divert people as they proceed into the fleecing pen. The MGM Grand has gone further: it spent hundreds of millions of dollars extra to build an adjacent but entirely separate amusement park, cramming seven rides (three involving fake rivers) and eight "themed areas" onto 33 acres, less than a 10th the size of Disney World.

The smart operators, such as Wynn, understand the proper Vegas meaning of family fun: people who won't take vacations without their children now have places to stick the kids while Mom and Dad pursue the essentially unwholesome act of squandering the family savings on cards and dice. "It's one thing for the place to be user-friendly to the whole family because the family travels together," Wynn says. "It's quite a different thing to sit down and dedicate creative design energy to build for children. I'm not, ain't gonna, not interested. I'm after Mom and Dad." Wynn's dolphins are just a '90s form of free Scotch and sodas, a cheap, subtler means of inducing people to leave their room and lose money.

But even if Vegas is not squeaky clean, even if its raison d'être remains something other than provoking a childlike sense of wonder, the place is no longer considered racy or naughty by most people. It seems incredible today that a book in the '60s about the city was called *Las Vegas, City of Sin?* The change in perception is mainly because Americans' collective tolerance for vulgarity has gone way, way up. Just a decade ago, "hell" and "damn" were the most offensive words permitted on broadcast TV; today the colloquialisms "butt" and "sucks" are in daily currency on all major networks. Characters on Fox sitcoms and MTV cartoon shows snicker about their erections, and the stars of *NYPD Blue* can call each other "asshole." Look at [TV talk-show hosts] Montel Williams and Geraldo. Listen to [radio shock-jock] Howard Stern.

In Vegas, Wynn actually gets a little defensive about his nudity-free shows ("Hey, I'm not afraid of boobies"), the streets are hookerless, and the best-known Vegas strip club, the Palomino, lies discreetly beyond the city limits. Meanwhile, at 116 Hooters restaurants in 30 states, the whole point is the battalion of bosomy young waitresses in tight-fitting tank tops who exist as fantasy objects for a clientele of high-testosterone frat boys and young bubbas. No wonder middle Americans find the idea of bringing kids along to Vegas perfectly appropriate. How ironic that two decades after Hunter Thompson's [1971] book *Fear and Loathing in Las Vegas*, countercultural ripple effects have so raised the American prudishness threshold that Las Vegas is considered no more unseemly than any other big city.

Sixteen years ago, Nevada was the only place in America where one could legally go to a casino, and there were just fourteen state lotteries. As recently as 1990, there were just three states with casinos, not counting those on Indian reservations; now there are nine. Lotteries have spread to 37 states. Indiana and five Mississippi River states have talked themselves into allowing gambling on riverboats—hey, it's not immoral, it's, you know, *historical*—and such floating casinos may soon be moored off Boston and in Philadelphia as well. Sensible, upright Minnesota, of all places, now has more casinos than Atlantic City. With only one state, Hawaii, retaining a ban on gambling, and with cable-TV oligarch John Malone interested in offering gambling on the information superhighway, Vegas doesn't seem sinful, just more entertaining and shameless.

And fortunate, especially in this age of taxophobia and budget freezes. The state of Nevada now derives half its public funds from gaming-related revenues—from voluntary consumption taxes, nearly all paid by out-of-staters. Nevadans pay no state income or inheritance tax. To craven political leaders elsewhere, this looks pretty irresistible: no pain, all gain, vigorish as fiscal policy. A new report from the Center for the Study of the States concluded, however, that "gambling cannot generally produce enough tax revenue to significantly reduce reliance on other taxes or to solve a serious state fiscal problem."

One of the defining features of Las Vegas has been its 24-hour commercial culture, which arose as a corollary to 24-hour casinos. Along with the University of Nevada's basketball team, it is the great source of civic pride. It is the salient urban feature first mentioned by Harvard-educated physician Mindy Shapiro about her adopted city: "You can buy a Cuisinart or drop off your dry cleaning at 4 in the morning!" The comic magician Penn Jillette, who was performing at Bally's last week, marvels, "There are no good restaurants, but at least they're open at 3 in the morning."

But Las Vegas' retail ceaselessness is no longer singular. These days around-the-clock restaurants and supermarkets are unremarkable in hyperconvenient America, and the information superhighway, even in its current embryonic state, permits people everywhere to consume saucy entertainment—

whether pay-per-view pornography or dating by modem with strangers—at any time of the day or night.

Las Vegas was created as the world's first experiential duty-free zone, a place dedicated to the anti-Puritan pursuit of instant gratification—no waiting, no muss, no fuss. In the '30s, Nevada was famous for its uniquely quick and easy marriage (and divorce) laws. And although a certain kind of demented Barbie and Ken still make it a point to stage their weddings in Las Vegas (158,470 people married there in 1992, a majority of them out-of-staters), it is now an atavistic impulse, since the marriage and divorce laws in the rest of the U.S. have long since caught up with Nevada's pioneering looseness.

When instant gratification becomes a supreme virtue, pop culture follows. Siegfried and Roy, the ur-Vegas magicians (imagine, if you dare, a hybrid of [flamboyant pianist] Liberace, Arnold Schwarzenegger, [magician] David Copperfield and [TV zoologist] Marlin Perkins) who perform 480 shows a year in their own theater at the Mirage, don't seem satisfied unless every trick is a show-stopper and every moment has the feel of a finale. In front of the new Treasure Island is a Caribbean-cum-Mediterranean faux village fronting a 65-ft.-deep "lagoon" in which a full-scale British man-of-war and pirate vessel every 90 minutes stage a battle with serious fires, major explosions, 22 actors, stirring music, a sinking ship. It is very impressive, completely satisfying—and gives spectators pretty much everything in 15 minutes, for free, that they go to certain two-hour, $65-a-seat Broadway musicals for.

In the '50s and '60s Vegas impresarios took a dying strain of vaudeville and turned it into a highly particular Vegas style. Gamblers from Duluth and Atlanta came to see only-in-Vegas entertainments: Sinatra, Streisand, stand-up comedians, the trash rococo of Liberace, both flaunting and denying his gayness; hot-ticket singer-dancers like Ann-Margret; and shows with whiffy themes that existed as mere pretexts for bringing out brigades of suggestively costumed young women jiggling through clouds of pastel-colored smoke as over-amped pop tunes blared. It was cheesy glamour, to be sure, but it was rare and one of a kind.

Precisely when did Vegas values start leaching deep into the American entertainment mainstream? Was it when Sammy

Davis Jr. got his own prime-time variety show on NBC in 1966, or a year later, when both [comedian] Jerry Lewis *and* Joey Bishop had network shows running? Or in the summer of 1969, when Elvis Presley staged his famous 14-show-a-week comeback gig in Vegas?

Whenever the change began, American show business is today so pervasively Vegasy that we hardly notice anymore. The arty, sexy French-Canadian circus Cirque du Soleil had its breakthrough run in Manhattan before decamping this year to Las Vegas, and neither venue seemed unnatural. Big rock-'n'-roll concerts nowadays are often as much about wowie-kazowie production values—giant video walls, neon, fire-works, suggestively costumed young men and women, clouds of pastel-colored smoke—as music. Michael Jackson's highly stylized shtick—the cosmetics, the wardrobe, the not-quite-dirty bumps and grinds, the Liberace-like gender-preference coyness—is so Vegas that the city embraced him at every turn: a Jackson impersonator is a star of the Riviera's long-running show *Splash;* Jackson plays a spaceship commander in one of Sega's new virtual-reality video games at the Luxor; and Siegfried and Roy got the real Jackson to compose and sing their show-closing theme song, *Mind Is the Magic.* And Madonna? Her just finished Girlie Show world tour, with its Vegas-style dancers and meretricious Vegas-style lighting, is precisely as pseudosexy in 1993 as shows at the Flamingo were in 1963—decadence lite.

Back when the Rat Pack ruled, Jackie Mason played Vegas and Edward Albee was on Broadway. Today essentially idea-free spectacle—*the Phantom of the Opera Cats*—dominates New York City's so-called legitimate theater, and stand-up comedy is ubiquitous. In the '90s, Friars Club comedians like Mason have hit Broadway shows, and Andrew Lloyd Webber's Broad-way musical *Starlight Express* has been permanently installed in the showroom of the Las Vegas Hilton. The crossbreeding seems complete. . . .

Last year 8 million of the city's 22 million visitors were un-der 40, and nearly half of those were under 30. When [the rock band] Soul Asylum, as part of the MTV-sponsored 1993 Al-ternative Nation tour, landed at its last U.S. stop in Las Vegas, the band deviated from its song list to belt out Vegasy tunes like *Mandy* and *Rhinestone Cowboy*. Luke Perry and Jason Priestley of [early '90s TV show] *Beverly Hills, 90210*, huge Tom Jones fans, recently flew to Vegas to see their hero sing, and members of the [rock group] Red Hot Chili Peppers went to Las Vegas to see and meet [singer] Julio Iglesias. "Suddenly the same things I was doing five years ago that were considered pure corn are now perceived to be in," says [perennial Las Vegas singer] Wayne Newton. "It's a wonderful satisfaction to finally be hip."

Long before this generation of young hipsters started reveling in the Vegas gestalt, certain intellectuals were taking seriously the city's no-holds-barred urban style. It was 25 years ago that a little-known architect and professor, Robert Venturi, returned to Yale with his two dozen student acolytes after a remarkable 10-day expedition to Las Vegas, where they stayed at the Stardust. His influential 1972 book, *Learning from Las Vegas*, immediately made Venturi famous as a heretical high-culture proponent for the ad hoc, populist design of the Strip—the giant neon signs, the kitschy architectural allusions to ancient Rome and the Old West, any zany kind of skin-deep picturesqueness. And a decade later, the fringe tendency became a full-fledged movement: Post-Modernism.

Today almost every big-city downtown has new skyscrapers that endeavor to look like old skyscrapers. Almost every suburb has a shopping center decorated with phony arches, phony pediments, phony columns. Two decades after Venturi proposed, with the intellectual's standard perverse quasi-affection, that Vegas could be a beacon for the nation's architecture, his manifesto had transformed America. Forget the Bauhaus [German school for architecture founded in 1919] and your house—it is the Vegas aesthetic, architecture as grandiose cartoon, that has become the American Establishment style. And so the splendidly pyramidal new Luxor and cubist new MGM Grand (both the work of local architect Veldon Simpson) do not seem so weird, since equally odd buildings now exist all over the place.

As it was being created in the '50s, Vegas' Strip was a mutant kind of American main drag, an absurdly overscaled Main Street for cars instead of people. Everywhere else in the country the shopping mall was replacing the traditional downtown.

But now the Strip in Las Vegas has come full circle, its vacant stretches filling in with so many new hotels and casinos that what had been the ultimate expression of car culture has masses of tourists *walking* from Bally's to Caesars to Treasure Island, and from the Luxor to the Excalibur to the MGM Grand. The Strip is virtually an old-fashioned Main Street.

Meanwhile malls, the fin-de-siècle scourge of genuine Main Streets, have become preposterous Vegasy extravaganzas themselves—themed, entertainment driven, all-inclusive, overwhelming. The West Edmonton Mall in Alberta, with its 119 acres of stores and restaurants and the world's largest indoor amusement park, pulled in 22 million people in 1992, as many as visited Las Vegas; and the 16-month-old Mall of America outside Minneapolis, with only 96 acres of money-spending opportunity and America's largest indoor amusement park, claimed 40 million visitors in its first year.

Yet even as the rest of America has become more and more like Las Vegas, life for Vegas residents as well as visitors is more thoroughly sugar-frosted with fantasy than anywhere else. "Our customers want a passive experience," says Wynn, "but romantic." Such as his ersatz South Seas restaurant, Kokomos ("Kokomos—this is *better* than Hawaii. There's no place in the South Pacific where the light is so perfect, so beautiful"). At the Mediterranean-themed resort Wynn envisions for the new Dunes site down the Strip, he has talked of creating a kind of raffish virtual Nazism: at a casino-restaurant modeled on Rick's casino-restaurant in *Casablanca* [1942 movie starring Humphrey Bogart], scenes from the movie would seamlessly blend with live actors playing Bogart and the movie's other characters among the paying customers.

The new Las Vegas has even fabricated a bit of ersatz old Las Vegas: along with its Oriental- and Bahamian-themed suites, the MGM offers rooms themed according to a decorator's Vegas ideal. The Sands, one of the last intact artifacts of the Rat Pack golden era, is being remodeled to within an inch of its life. "We're going to theme, definitely," the hotel's p.r. spokeswoman said as work was beginning late last year. "But we don't know what the themes are yet.". . .

The theming; Liberace and Michael Jackson and Siegfried and Roy; the water gluttony [per capita water usage in Las Vegas is 343 gallons per day, 58% higher than Los Angeles]; the refusal to build schools and police stations. It is fair to say that Las Vegas is in denial, which probably explains the local predilection for smarmy euphemism. From Wayne Newton on down, every man in Vegas calls every woman a lady. One of the local abortion clinics is called A Lady's Needs. Signs all over McCarran Airport declare it a nonsmoking building, yet just as noticeable as the banks of slot machines is the reek of old cigarettes. It strikes almost no one as ironic that the patron of the M.B. Dalitz Religious School is the late Moe Dalitz, the celebrated gangster.

It is understandable that the citizens are a bit embarrassed by their criminal founding fathers (Steve Wynn calls the Dunes "the original home of tinhorns and scumbags"), but the mixed feelings go beyond the mob. Last year Davy-O Thompson got zoning-board approvals to establish his haircutting salon, A Little Off the Top, where the female stylists were dressed in frilly teddies or paste-on breast caps and panties. But the board of cosmetology denied him a license an hour before he was set to open, citing concerns over "safety" and "hygiene." (He was eventually allowed to operate.) A similar protest contributed to the demise recently of a car wash featuring women in thong bikinis.

"We Las Vegans have been living under the stigma of Sin City for so long that we are desperate to prove that this is a very conservative, God-fearing, average American community that just happens to have gambling," explains Under Sheriff Eric Cooper, who along with his boss, Sheriff John Moran, has been waging a 10-year antivice campaign. "The best thing that ever happened was when the Baptists had their convention here four years ago." The category of "Escort Services" is no longer listed in the local Yellow Pages.

It isn't just sex. Las Vegans are even ambivalent about gambling. Political discourse often revolves around keeping casinos away from decent people's homes. The promotional video produced by the Nevada Development Authority makes no mention at all of casinos. Even when a casino is a part of a new development, it is described as something else. Jack Sommer's Mountain Spa, the post pseudo-Mediterranean resort about to start construction, will have a small "European-style" casino. But, says Sommer, "it's not really a *casino*. I call it a gaming amenity."

Semantic nuance, it turns out, is important. "They don't see themselves as gamblers," says Steve Wynn of the new tourists he is attracting. "They think of themselves as folks who are on vacation, and while they are there—hey, let's put some money in the slot machine." Wynn hired screenwriter Jim Hart (*Hook, Bram Stoker's Dracula*) to write a one-hour family-adventure TV movie (NBC, Jan. 23 [1994]) set at Treasure Island, and while Hart says the movie reaffirms family values and he flew his children out during production, he understands the place has an intrinsically dark edge. "You can come out for 24 hours and lose the tuition," he says. "There are a lot of desperate characters here."

For while the city is no longer the "Genet vision of hell" that John Gregory Dunne described in his book *Vegas: A Memoir of a Dark Season* 20 years ago, it is still, for the moment, a stranger place than Omaha or Sacramento or Worcester or even Atlantic City, if only because there are so many cheerfully offered temptations to lose the tuition and so many normal-looking people flirting feverishly with that risk. The mobs on the casino floors are in a kind of murmuring trance, each middle-aged housewife or young lawyer at the slots or the poker tables mentally grappling with a nonstop flow of insane hunches and wishful superstitions, continuously driven to unworthy leaps of faith that result in unwarranted bursts of self-esteem (*Blackjack!*) or self-loathing (*Craps!*).

Wynn understands the shadowy core of Las Vegas. "There will never come a day when [potential visitors] say, 'Should it be Orlando or should it be Las Vegas?' Those are two different moods. We think of our vacation in more romantic, personal terms. We're looking for sensual, extended gratification." In other words, Disney World is about tightly scripted smile-button fun for the kids; Las Vegas, despite the new theme-park accessories, remains the epicenter of the American id, still desperate to overpay schmaltzy superstars like Barbra Streisand, still focused on the darker stirrings of chance and liquor and sex.

If it is now acceptable for the whole family to come along to Las Vegas, that's because the values of America have changed, not those of Las Vegas. Deviancy really has been defined down. The new hang-loose, all-American embrace of Las Vegas is either a sign that Americans have liberated themselves from troublesome old repressions and moralist hypocrisies, or else one more symptom of the decline of Western civilization. Or maybe both.

Baiting Gamblers with Rock and Roll

Elizabeth Gilbert

In the 1990s, the gambling industry marketed casinos to a younger, hipper crowd in an effort to alter gambling's image as an activity for retirees and win the patronage of a coveted group of consumers. These efforts paid off in Las Vegas, which reemerged at the close of the twentieth century as an exciting place for young people to vacation. The gambling capital's popular resurgence was largely responsible for bringing a new generation of gamblers into casinos around the country.

In the following article written for *Spin* magazine in the mid-1990s, Elizabeth Gilbert describes how the Hard Rock Casino in Las Vegas employs a rock and roll theme—rock star memorabilia on the walls and slot machines, etc.—to appeal directly to younger gamblers. The casino exploits the "outlaw culture of rock" to sell gambling to suburban vacationers, in the author's opinion. Gilbert is a regular contributor to *GQ* magazine and the author of *The Last American Man*.

ONE FINE AFTERNOON, I AM SUNBATHING BY THE swimming pool of the swank new Hard Rock Hotel and Casino in Las Vegas, Nevada. I am enjoying a cocktail when a Hootie & the Blowfish tune comes on through the outdoor speakers: "Only Wanna Be with You."

The song is not a favorite and I dive into the pool to avoid listening. But the Hard Rock Hotel and Casino pool is

■

equipped with underwater speakers, so I hear the same Hootie tune, aquatically amplified whenever my head goes under. I climb out of the pool and dry off to the strains of Hootie. I walk into the hotel through the Hard Rock Athletic Club, where guests are exercising to the Hootie beat. Past the Hard Rock merchandise store, where shoppers are shopping to Hootie. Through the glittery casino itself, where Hootie pumps out loudly over the clanging slot machines. Into the elevator, for a smooth Hootie ride. Safe in my room, I pick up the phone to call room service. They put me on hold, where I find Hootie coming through the receiver. Hootie wafting in on a breeze through my open window. Hootie slipping faintly under my door, like a smell.

Hootie, everywhere. Everywhere Hootie.

Where Rock Meets Gambling

The Hard Rock Hotel and Casino can be found on Paradise Road in Las Vegas. By most standards, it's not small (17 acres, 340 rooms, and a $100 million price tag), but it's pretty dinky for this town. The Excalibur Casino-Hotel boasts 4,032 rooms. The MGM Grand has 5,000. To the real big-shot Vegas hoteliers, a 340-room place is basically a Motel 6. What's more, the Hard Rock Casino contains a mere 800 slot machines. A corporate gambling giant like Harrah's picks casinos bigger than this out of its stool every morning.

So this is a small story for Las Vegas. But it's a big story for the Hard Rock Cafe. The new casino complex stands as the first serious aberration in a 24-year pattern of marketing mega-success. Like all good franchises, the Hard Rock owes its stability to a consistent formula. Until now, it hasn't budged from that formula. Wherever they are in the world, Hard Rock Cafes deliver music memorabilia on the walls, classic rock in the air, expensive hamburgers on the plate, and piles of T-shirts in the company store. In return, the customers (about 60 percent of whom are tourists) provide Hard Rock America with approximately $115 million a year.

Peter Morton, founder of the empire and father of this new casino venture, has said, "I created the Hard Rock Cafes because I wanted people to have a place to go where they could experience the fun of rock'n'roll."

This is an important statement, although to some of us it might seem a little odd. Is rock'n'roll inherently fun? For that matter, is gambling? The real connection between rock and gambling is not "fun" but their juicy, shared histories of corruption and recklessness. These are two dark American traditions—sexy, dirty, painful, shot through with vice.

So how does a corporation combine these two beautifully tainted cultures to create a friendly setting, sanitized and harmless enough for any suburban consumer?

First step: Eliminate any irony.

I am momentarily paralyzed by what I see when checking in at the Hard Rock. Right above the front desk, big, cheerful brass letters spell out, HERE WE ARE NOW, ENTERTAIN US.

Underneath, smaller letters note, almost parenthetically, KURT COBAIN.

"Enjoy your stay!" chirps the desk clerk. "Have fun!"

Bogus or Awesome?

The room keys at the Hard Rock Hotel come in a tiny folder that is marked ALL ACCESS, in the manner of a VIP backstage pass. The poker chips in the casino are stamped with images of the Red Hot Chili Peppers, Jimi Hendrix, Tom Petty, and Bob Seger. The lights in the hallways of the Hard Rock Casino are shaded by Zildjian drum cymbals. The elevators are lined in black studded faux-leather, so you sort of feel like you're riding up and down in [rock musician] Tommy Lee's pants. The T-shirts in the merchandise store are displayed on roadie cases. The do-not-disturb signs in the hotel room read I HEAR YA KNOCKIN' BUT YA CAN'T COME IN. One can even order a cocktail called "Da Doo Ron Ron Rum Runner." At the end of their stay, guests are asked to report whether the hotel was "bogus" or "awesome." The casino carpets are decorated with musical notes and the room drapes have a pretty pattern of interwoven guitars.

In the interest of taste, not every rock-theme opportunity has been seized. The cocktail waitresses, for instance, are not referred to as "groupies" (although they are dressed like them). The pool is not shaped like Keith Richards's kidney. Nor is it shaped like a guitar. But 250 of the slot machines do have Fender guitar-neck pull handles, and others have names like

"Better Be Good to Me" and "Take the Money and Run." This brings us to a discussion of the really special slot machines.

There are two types of custom-designed slot machines at the Hard Rock Casino. One is the Purple Haze slot machine. The other is the Sex Pistols slot machine. The Sex Pistols slot machine, decorated with Union Jacks, pictures a snarling Sid Vicious above the ANARCHY IN VEGAS! Below this is an explanation: THIS MACHINE ACCEPTS 1, 5, 10, 20, 50, 100 DOLLAR BILLS.

The Purple Haze slot machine pictures [guitarist] Jimi Hendrix on his knees in supplication, his head thrown back and his arms spread messianically. Spilling from his hands are the figures $1, $5, $10, $20, $50, $100. A note adds, ONE PURPLE HAZE SYMBOL DOUBLES WINNING COMBINATION.

I am examining these machines on a Friday morning when a bus tour arrives and unloads its passengers. The passengers, tourists who tell me they are from "the greater Denver area," seem mostly to be retired people in their 60s and 70s. They proceed to explore the casino in small clusters. Their uniform of choice is the jogging suit, and these jogging suits are impressive creations, vividly colored and decorated with metallic beads and regal gold stitching. The retirees move through the Hard Rock Casino like a resplendent flotilla of yachts, their jogging suits billowing in the air conditioning like sails.

A brittle, aging gentleman peels away from his group and sits down at the Purple Haze slot machine. He has a $10 roll of quarters, which I watch him systematically lose. Bad luck for me. I was hoping he would win, so I could make a joke about Hendrix vomiting out the winnings.

"Do you like Jimi Hendrix?" I ask.

He says politely, "I'm very sorry, ma'am, but I don't know who that is."

Then I tell him that I like his jogging suit, which I do. It is imprinted with maps.

"Thank you," he says. "These are flight maps of the American Middle West. And I'm proud to wear them."

Targeting the Forty-Nine-Year Generation

"We are an oasis of cool in Las Vegas.". . .

Morton's Hard Rock Casino publications continually

promise a Vegas for a New Generation—a theme echoed in numerous newspaper articles, like one that ran recently in the *New York Times* headlined "Hard Rock Cafe Draws the Young to Las Vegas."

"We get a real young party crowd in here," a security guard confirms. And a boyish bellhop says, "Every day at the Hard Rock is like spring break."

Well, perhaps like a spring break *reunion.*

The staff is certainly young and hip, but, surprisingly often, the clientele is not. Particularly not during daylight hours. Having been promised a crowd of young rockers, I'm amazed at how many people are, well, Mick Jagger's age. Or even older. And it's not the hippest cross-section of America, either. Most gamblers could be described by a term I dislike, but which rhymes with "light rash." (One good ol' boy, after winning $400 at the craps table, brags to me, "Shake the hand of a man who's buying himself a brand new three-wheeler ATV.")

I see many more families than I expected, as well as seniors, and the decidedly upper-middle-aged. Trying to make sense of this, I start asking people why they like the Hard Rock Casino. Whatever their age or background, they have the same answer.

A 21-year-old college student from Michigan tells me, "This casino is for our generation, you know? For people like me and you, who want something really cool."

A 38-year-old Minnesota landscaper says, "It's good for young people like us. You know, for our generation."

A 47-year-old Nashville sales clerk explains, "I like it because it's targeted at our generation. You know, the younger crowd."

A "60-year-old granny" says, "This place is great. All this memorabilia you see around here is for my generation. The younger set. The rock'n'roll generation."

At least the 76-year-old woman I meet in the merchandise shop doesn't claim that the Hard Rock Casino represents her generation, too. Instead, she says, she is shopping for her 11-year-old granddaughter, who "just loves this place."

"Why?" I ask.

"Well," the woman answers, "the Hard Rock is really created for her generation, after all."

Just check that out. A generation that includes a sixth-grader at one end and a 60-year-old at the other is a mighty 49-year generation. Most people wouldn't even call that a generation. Most people would go ahead and call that a half-century. You have to salute Hard Rock founder Peter Morton on this. He's got a half-century worth of American consumers convinced that he's representing them, and that they are all young, all hip, all rockers. *That* is marketing.

The New Allure

Let's take a moment to examine recent Las Vegas history. Vegas remains a dirty and permissive town, but it is not nearly so dirty and permissive as it once was. Once, there were no speed limits here, no sales tax, no closing time for bars. If you got in trouble with the Mafia, the cops would never hear about it. There were no waiting periods for marriages, no regulations on gambling, no pasties for strippers. This naughtiness went unchecked for several decades, until the federal government decided to get tough with organized crime in the late 1970s. Key people went to jail, most of the Mob left Las Vegas, and the sinfulness was considerably truncated.

Then came another devastating event: In 1976, gambling was legalized in Atlantic City. Vegas was no longer the only game in town. These days, of course, there is competition everywhere. Now you can gamble legally in northern Connecticut, aboard Midwestern riverboats, and in Biloxi, Mississippi, among other seductive places. So why should anyone go all the way to Nevada anymore? Las Vegas needed a new allure.

In the last three years, theme casinos have come to the desert. The goal was to transform this sinful city into a family-oriented vacation spot. It has worked. Nobody could have imagined this happening a generation ago, when the fellas who ran Vegas all had the middle name "The." (One local taxi driver tells me, "Suddenly, the busiest times of the year out here are Christmas, Thanksgiving, and Easter. Can you believe that shit? People bring their kids to Vegas for *Easter*?")

In fact, Las Vegas has become a lot like Branson, Missouri, with slot machines: an expensive tourist destination where real experience has been replaced by processed "experience." One of the new theme casinos is Treasure Island, which boasts a live pirate-ship battle six times each evening in the lagoon out front. The Luxor is a huge copy of the Great Pyramid with the Sphinx nearby, and the parking attendants dress like Egyptian slaves. The MGM Grand is modeled after the Emerald City of Oz. My favorite, however, is the Excalibur—a huge, tacky castle, surrounded by a fake moat (which is spanned by a moving sidewalk, basically defeating the purpose of a moat). As you approach the Excalibur, a recorded voice in a half-assed English accent announces, "Hear ye, hear ye! This is King Arthur speaking! Prepare to transport yourself back to the days of King Arthur, where you can enjoy 100,000 square feet of gaming excitement!"

There is a general laziness to these theme casinos. For instance, there's no landscaping around them, because nobody cares. You have a trillion-dollar building set in the middle of a cracked, dirty, unevenly paved parking lot. Doesn't matter. Everyone's trying to get inside anyhow. Once you're inside the Excalibur, the medieval experience really amounts to nothing. They stick a fake knight-in-armor by a slot machine here and there, to help you feel "transported." Families in swimming suits walk around sipping ice-cream drinks out of fake gold chalices. It's like the owners are saying, "Here's your stinking castle, folks. Now start gambling."

Marketing Science

The Hard Rock Casino looks lazy, too, at first glance. The walls are covered with rock memorabilia, but the stuff isn't presented with any sense of order, context, or value. Every artist is given the same presentation: Neil Young next to Garth Brooks next to Metallica next to Elvis. The entrance to the casino is flanked by two huge panoramic display cases. On the left are Madonna collectibles. On the right are Buddy Holly collectibles.

There's no attempt at chronology. There's no sense of the artist. Rock star clothing is starched, pressed, and hung on faceless mannequins. Even [rock musician] Courtney Love's dress looks clean. All the leather jackets and guitars start to look alike, until there's no difference between White Zombie, Bruce Springsteen, Billy Idol, and the Cranberries.

Everything appears completely random, but of course it

isn't. There are no accidents here. The Hard Rock Casino, like the rest of the new Vegas, is the product of marketing science. If there is only one plastic knight-in-armor in each bathroom at the Excalibur, it is because market research has determined that consumers want only a hint of medieval ambience amid modern amenities, not the real deal complete with sputtering torches and urine-soaked straw on the floor.

Similarly, if the Hard Rock has grouped together rock artists and elements of rock history that seem to have no connection, it is because American consumers have done the same. Rock'n'roll is cool. Super-successful, million-selling rock'n'roll artists—of all eras, in all styles—are extremely cool. The concept doesn't have to be any more specific than that to work. The outlaw culture of rock long ago became a highly desirable commodity. Obviously, the Hard Rock corporation didn't create this situation. They did, however, recognize it, co-opt it, and market it expertly.

"We have succeeded," Peter Morton says, "by trying to give the people something we believe they want." Evidently he is right again. The Hard Rock Casino turns away about 300 people seeking rooms every weekend, and merchandise sales are ahead of projections by an amazing 75 percent.

The crowds at the Hard Rock Casino pass the archival displays without focusing on them, but I spend a lot of time staring at the collected memorabilia, seeking a reaction in myself. What is this stuff meant to evoke? Why was this particular item chosen? But the longer I look, the more I miss the point. Rock'n'roll is cool. Nothing more is being said here. Andy Warhol once described the Hard Rock Empire as "the Smithsonian of rock'n'roll." But with all due respect to Warhol, it's really just a wax museum.

The following is a selection of items emblazoned with the famous Hard Rock emblem that are currently available at the Hard Rock Casino merchandise store:

T-shirts, baby clothes, backpacks, bikinis, golf balls, golf-club covers, beer mugs, socks, picture frames, pillowcases, collector's-edition plates, dice, mugs, key chains, wallets, hats, leather jackets, denim jackets, wine, olive oil, and a mysterious amber fluid in a little tiny vial labeled HARD ROCK DESERT GOLD BATH GEL.

Depressingly, the consumers who seem to buy the most stuff are those who already seem completely merchandise-saturated. They're already covered with junk, having dressed themselves in advertisements for Planet Hollywood, Nike, Reebok, Coca-Cola, Marlboro, Joe Camel, and the collected works of Mr. Walt Disney.

Amid all that product placement, it's a relief to see some true individuality in one chubby couple. They are wearing white undershirts, upon which they've written their own messages in laundry pen. I follow the couple through the store, but they buy nothing, only increasing my admiration.

His T-shirt says, THE FASTEST WAY TO A MAN'S HEART IS THROUGH HIS FLY.

Hers says, I'M TALKING AND I CAN'T SHUT UP.

Anything Goes?

After nightfall at the Hard Rock Casino, the crowd changes. The population shifts to a younger, preppier group of individuals. The uniform goes from jogging suits to khakis. The girls wear pretty makeup and prom-night hair. The boys wear oxford shirts and baseball caps. Some of the freakier folks have goatees. It is a very, very white crowd. The blasting music is exactly what kids in my high school were listening to a decade ago: "Jack and Diane," "Night Moves," "Dear Mr. Fantasy."

One of the pit bosses told me earlier that a lot of the nighttime clients are "rich Californians," but everyone I talk to seems to be from the American Middle West. Chicago and its suburbs are particularly well-represented. I can't figure out where any of these kids got the cash to risk at the blackjack table, so I start asking them. In explanation, I am handed a lot of business cards.

In a few hours, I collect business cards from sales representatives, accountants, engineers, marketing managers, public-relations officers, bankers, and brokers. No doctors. One lawyer. A few young college students with fake IDs confess that they slipped past the security guards, but are too nervous to try to get a drink. Everyone is having fun. Just ask them.

I try to interview people, but they can explain little except that they are having fun. They tell me rock'n'roll is the greatest. They tell me gambling is the greatest. The Hard Rock

Casino is really the greatest. When I ask what makes the place great, they tend to pump their fists in the air and shout, "*Rock-'n'roll*, man!"

But the only people I see all weekend who actually look like rockers are the *SPIN* photographer, Geoffroy, and his assistant, Pierrot—two French guys in leather pants, with skinny hips and cigarettes. Pierrot looks particularly authentic, spending much of the weekend drinking and not sleeping and walking around the casino unshaven, with messy hair, saying, "This ain't rock'n'roll! This eez genocide!"

The Hard Rock party crowd gives Pierrot a lot of raised-eyebrow looks, like, "What's with *that* guy?" I slowly begin to realize they are afraid of him.

For example. I am talking to a frat boy on spring break from Seton Hall. I ask him why he likes the Hard Rock Casino. He gives me the arm-pump thing. He says, "This place is wild, man! Anything goes here! Totally fucking crazy!"

I point to Pierrot, and ask, "What do you think of that guy?"

The frat boy frowns. He says, "That guy's weird, man."

Missing the Mob

"This ain't Vegas," Randy is complaining. "This is Disneyland."

I meet Randy at the Hard Rock Casino on the same night I am trying to ask people what they like about the place. Randy is a lifelong resident of Las Vegas. His father has worked at the old New Frontier Inn Casino for 30 years, and Randy is himself a craps dealer at a major Strip hotel.

"I couldn't get a job at this place," Randy says, gesturing at the Hard Rock gaming tables. "Are you kidding me? It's too uptight, too corporate, too tight-ass. They do drug tests on all the employees, and check police records and IRS records. Also, I'm over 30, and they want younger, more innocent people dealing here. Pisses me off, too, because I taught the floor manager here how to deal craps."

Randy is strictly old-school Vegas. He grew up with gangsters' kids and dealers' kids and showgirls' kids. Like all the guys in the 'hood, he thought he would grow up to be a big player, too.

"In the old days," Randy says, "a gambler could walk into the Horseshoe Casino and lay a half-million down on a single throw of the dice and—win or lose—nobody would bat an eye. The Horseshoe would 'fade' any bet. Nowadays, you've got these corporations running Vegas, building these stupid theme-park casinos, cutting every corner, so tourists can come with their kids. Ask anybody who grew up here. Vegas sucks now. It was better when the Mob ran things. It was better when the boys had it."

Randy looks around him at the Hard Rock crowd with pronounced disdain. "And look at this place. A bunch of college kids from Kansas, laying down $2 bets. All this fake rock-'n'roll bullshit. There's no high rollers here. There's no glamour here. These are bozos who show up with a shirt and a $20 bill, and they don't change either one all week."

The next night, Randy takes me and the *SPIN* photographers on a tour of old Vegas, or what's left of it. We drive around in his late-model Cadillac, blasting tunes, drinking beer, and listening to Randy's stories about the old days, when Vegas was still "mobbed up." We drive past the Flamingo and the Tropicana, and the original glimmering Strip. We drive past all the small, old fleabag motels, like the Pollyanna, the Carnival, and the Normandie (with its sad neon sign reading HIGHLY RECOMMENDED BY OWNER). We end up at the Horseshoe Casino, where the dealers are shrewd old men and the gamblers are even shrewder and older.

Loathing the Hard Rock

Around midnight, I do the only thing a girl can do when trying to understand Las Vegas. I call Hunter S. Thompson, who fathered gonzo journalism back in the '70s with his book *Fear and Loathing in Las Vegas.*

"Hunter," I say, "I'm at the Horseshoe Casino in Vegas."

"I can't hear you very well," he says. Which is mutual. Thompson tends to swallow the last three words of every sentence, and the slot machines in the Horseshoe are loud.

I say, "What do you think of the Hard Rock Casino?"

"I like it," Thompson mumbles.

"Honestly? Why?"

"Because it answers to the private needs of the individual.

It's tasteful and clean. It offers the kind of variety that people like me need."

I can't believe what I'm hearing, and say, "I can't believe what I'm hearing."

"You just called for an argument," Thompson says.

"No!" I protest. "I called for a consensus! I think it's a heartless place. I don't think it has anything to do with Vegas or rock'n'roll. I like it better here at the dirty old Horseshoe Casino."

"Well, girlie, when you get to be my age, you'll understand the wisdom of what I'm saying."

I tell Thompson I am concerned about the sanitizing of America. Disney has recently moved to Times Square, and is building a family haven there, of all places. And now Vegas is becoming a second Orlando. What is happening to the dark, unsavory neighborhoods of this nation? Where will people go for vice?

"Girlie," Thompson says kindly. "You can't live like that forever. You can't be that flagrant and decadent 24 hours a day, the way Vegas used to be. Bugsy Siegel is dead. You have to clean up eventually. And the Hard Rock is clean."

I ask Thompson one more thing. "But, Hunter?" I say. "Don't you miss it? Don't you miss all the dirty stuff?"

After a long moment, he answers in an amused and wistful tone. "Oh, yeah. Absolutely."

A Shine to Business

Back at the Hard Rock Casino, it's now four in the morning. People are still gambling. There is a faint whiff of screwdriver-scented vomit by the elevator doors. I talk to a young security guard, and he says, "I don't know anything about how Las Vegas used to be, but I like it better now. I understand that it used to be a real dump. Apparently, it was really sleazy."

He is standing in front of the Kurt Cobain display case. Inside is a guitar, a jacket, and some photographs. The Kurt Cobain display case is equipped with two long slits in the glass, so fans can slide messages inside. The display is therefore littered with poems to Cobain, sketches of Cobain, letters for Cobain, etc. It's become a shrine. But some clever local entrepreneurs also slide their business cards inside. On this particular night, the shrine is advertising a divorce lawyer, a tattooist, a florist, and a taxi service.

Cobain's display case is the only one I see in the Hard Rock Casino that is not sealed. I can't help wondering whether the slits were a corporate decision, whether someone specifically designed this case to collect these fans' messages, to add some pathos. This strikes me as exploitative. So I write, on a piece of notebook paper, "This is exploitative." I slide the paper through one of the slits.

By the next morning, my message is gone. The business cards, however, remain.

The Return of "Sin City"

Jonah Goldberg

Large corporations broadened the appeal of Las Vegas—formerly regarded as "Sin City," the nation's capital of booze, sex, and gambling—by restyling it in the 1990s as a family-friendly destination complete with amusement parks and day care facilities. During the same period, however, casinos sprang up in states across the country, reducing the need to travel to Las Vegas for gambling. In the following article, Jonah Goldberg maintains that Las Vegas has gone back to promoting itself as a place where normally upright citizens can indulge in sinful pleasures, aiming to regain its unique stature as a place outside the mainstream of American society. The new Las Vegas sleaze, characterized by nude revues and large strip clubs, appears just as manufactured and "corporate" as the city's aborted appeal to families, in the author's opinion. Goldberg is a regular contributor to the conservative magazine *National Review* and editor-at-large for *National Review Online*.

"ARE YOU GOING TO WRITE ME A CHECK?" THE buxom headliner at the Luxor hotel's "Midnight Fantasy" asks me. "No," I mumble as I put away my pen, a bit distracted because she's wearing cowboy chaps that offer a view of her largely theoretical underwear. I'm taking notes during her show and I guess when a Vegas showgirl sees a pen, she assumes it's to write her a check. She asks my name and repeats

∎

Jonah Goldberg, "Living in Sin: Fantasy and Reality in Today's Las Vegas," *National Review*, vol. LIV, May 20, 2002, pp. 35–37. Copyright © 2002 by National Review, Inc., 215 Lexington Ave., New York, NY 10016. Reproduced by permission.

it for the whole audience. Then she instructs me: "Move your leg, honey." I comply and uncross my legs which, like my arms, had been constricted in a pretzel of uncomfortable body language: I hate shows, I hate audience participation, I hate *this*. She sits in my lap and sings to me and I ponder how I can kill myself without drawing any further attention.

Dinner Hour Fantasy

When she's done, she sashays back to the stage, turns coquettishly toward me—so as to ensure that her exposed derriere, shining in the spotlight, "faces" me through her chaps—and asks, "Would you like to see some *more* cowgirls, Jonah?" She doesn't wait for my answer and a parade of showgirls returns to the stage to lip-sync another spate of '80s hits, like Billy Idol's "Flesh for Fantasy."

Now, when it comes to topless women, one need not be an "if you've seen two, you've seen 'em all" kind of guy to find this show relentlessly boring. Despite the playbill's promise— "See every dreaming or waking fantasy you've ever had come to life"—ten minutes in and I'm sucking the last dregs of scotch off the ice cubes in my glass like it was an antidote to a neurotoxin.

But not everyone feels that way. Shortly after the cowgirl gets off my lap, I catch the eye of one envious older gentleman. Grinning, he gives me a thumbs-up, but holds it low by his hip so his wife doesn't see it. In fact, the audience is full of married couples; the stand-up comic who comes out halfway through the show takes one look at the crowd and says, "Look at all the married couples, this could be a cruise."

He's right. Indeed, a large number of folks in the audience look like they might receive a lot of solicitation mail from AARP [senior-citizen group]. It's impossible to know exactly how many of them came here after loading up on the early-bird senior-citizen special at Denny's, but few seem to have caught on to the irony that this is the 8:30 P.M. showing of "Midnight Fantasy." In fact, there is no midnight showing of "Midnight Fantasy," but apparently "Dinner Hour Fantasy" didn't have the right oomph.

This, apparently, is the future of Vegas. "Sin City," as countless headline writers have noted, "is back." Up and down the Strip, the skyline is dominated by huge, multistory video billboards featuring images of what would have passed for soft porn a generation ago. In my hotel, the MGM Grand, every elevator features a large sign for their nude revue, "La Femme." Small children, old ladies, junior-high-school soccer teams: Everyone sees the same butt—with just enough frilly thong to keep it legal—right over the floor-indicator.

It's a carnival of female flesh, year-round. Over 1,000 naked women perform in public on any given evening. Harrah's offers "Skintight," starring Vanna Lace—whose election as "Miss Nude World" was not, presumably, a reward for reading to the blind. A nightclub called "Skin" is scheduled to open in May; it will feature women shaking their groove thing on platforms while mermaids swim nude in a giant fish tank.

Las Vegas is making a conscious effort to shed the "family-friendly" reputation it earned in the last decade, and don the more risqué rep of yesteryear. The Old Vegas was not a place you wanted to take your kids to—the Dunes hotel offered topless dancing in the 1950s. But that all started to change when Steve Wynn opened the Mirage in 1989. Wynn, who should be given as much credit for creating the "new" Vegas as Bugsy Siegel got for creating the old one, all but declared that he wanted to steal tourists from traditional bring-the-whole-family venues. Declaring the Mirage a "Disney/fantasy experience," Wynn put a shark tank behind the check-in desk and set up a day-care center for hotel guests. "Neon is cheap," he told *USA Today*. "It's yesterday's Las Vegas."

Vegas quickly became an entertainment mecca for family travelers. In 1991 Kirk Kerkorian broke ground on a billion-dollar project: a 5,000-room hotel with an amusement park roughly the size of Vatican City and an adjoining sports arena bigger than Madison Square Garden. In short order, New York New York, The Luxor, the Venetian, and a host of other theme hotels went up, almost as quickly as the old ones with cigarette-stained drapes and otherwise-stained mattresses came down.

Wynn's bet paid off. By 1994, *Time* magazine's cover called Las Vegas an "All-American City." *U.S. News & World Report* featured a similar cover: "Sin City No More." In 1998, Wynn opened the Bellagio, a $1.6 billion luxury hotel complete with

New Facade, Same Old Racket

Opulent beyond anything Las Vegas has ever known, the new Strip mega-resorts, with their $400-a-night accommodations, house world-famous gourmet cafés, and fashionable international boutiques with such tenants as Armani, Chanel, Lagerfeld, Hermès, and Gucci. The new casino complexes, self-contained bazaars of luxury, mark Las Vegas's appeal to the richest and increasingly prosperous top 5 percent of America's population. Though the city still draws and depends upon the general populace—striving "to sell its elitism to the masses," as one local journalist puts it—it has always been a place where ordinary people come to feel extraordinary. But now that the preponderance of visitors cannot afford the sumptuous new rooms and restaurants, they troop through the new resorts and their enclosed malls with Paris street names or Italian marble walkways, peering at the window displays and ornate lobbies as if they were passersby in the exclusive blocks of some Gilded Age city.

Yet beyond the glamour and massiveness of the once again reinvented city, its essence never changes. The new corridors of affluence and pretension still lead to the gigantic casinos that are the heart of the matter, the reason for all the rest. However discreetly lit or adorned, electronically encased or programmed, the racket works now as it always has, with the single ultimate purpose of taking the public's money in a manner no other industry in the world can match. Those who see that reality most clearly, the few who knew the old Las Vegas, are unfazed by the new facade. "A joint's a joint," says a casino manager who came to the city with Meyer Lansky.

Sally Denton and Roger Morris, *The Money and the Power: The Making of Las Vegas and Its Hold on America, 1947–2000*. New York: Knopf, 2001.

a mini-museum with roughly $300 million worth of paintings by Degas, van Gogh, Picasso, and Matisse. You could still find the world's largest rhinestone at the Liberace Museum if you wanted, but clearly this was an appeal to a different clientele.

The Malleable Metropolis

The concept of the New Vegas was shockingly simple: Every place you went to was supposed to remind you of someplace else. Caesars Palace, of course, is Classical Rome. The Luxor is a giant Pyramid on the outside and Ancient Egypt on the inside. Treasure Island is self-explanatory. The Venetian boasts actual gondola rides on man-made canals; New York New York looks like the iconic Gotham skyline on the outside and has a cavern of faux–New York ethnic eateries on the inside; the Paris showcases a nightly performance at which the entire beret-wearing staff surrenders *en masse* to busloads of German tourists every hour on the half-hour.

Okay, just kidding about that last part, but you get the point. Las Vegas had no culture of its own—at least none worth advertising—so it ripped off—er, borrowed—other people's. It was Epcot Center with gambling and more cleavage.

In all its brilliance and shamelessness, Las Vegas really did become in the 1990s a classic American enterprise. In *The Money and the Power: The Making of Las Vegas and Its Hold on America*, Sally Denton and Roger Morris write that Las Vegas "is a city in the middle of nowhere that is the world's most popular destination. It is a fount of enormous wealth that produces nothing. Once thought the society's aberrant city, it is not just newly respectable but proves to have been an archetype all along."

And now, true to its role as the malleable metropolis of American hedonism, Las Vegas is changing again. The success of Steve Wynn's Vegas was predicated on getting the most customers with the most money to spend to come to Vegas. This meant expanding the city's appeal to families with children. The idea wasn't, Wynn insisted, to become "family-friendly" so much as to be friendly to people who wouldn't come to Vegas unless their family could come too.

Alan Feldman is the vice president of MGM-Mirage Casinos, and worked with Wynn when he opened the Mirage. He says that most of the razzle-dazzle—the erupting volcanoes and so on—was never intended to entertain children, so much as make adults "feel like kids again." After all, he notes defensively, "the explosions at the pirate battle scare little kids." And Kerkorian's massive Wizard of Oz–themed amusement park? "That is now seen as a decision of great error." He's certainly right on that score. The place is closed to everything but tumbleweeds.

Faux Naughtiness

As countless casino executives have noted in industry journals, whether it was a family-friendly or friendly-to-families policy, it worked. Vegas's customer base grew from 18 million a year in 1989 to over 35 million today [2002], with these visitors spending more and staying longer.

So why abandon the policy? The media were quick to report that the nudie girls started coming out after [the terrorist attacks on] September 11, 2001, which had, in fact, delivered a terrible blow to the city's business. But Feldman and other Vegas hands dismiss this theory, noting that these highly produced shows were in the works long before the terrorist attacks.

There are actually at least three interrelated reasons why sin is making such a comeback at the big casinos (it never left the more modest establishments). The first is a national trend. Gambling is now everywhere in the United States: Thirty-eight out of 50 states allow it. It was thought, at first, that this trend would cut into Vegas's profits, but that hasn't been the case. "It's like golf," a pit-boss explains to me. "If you really develop a love for the game at your local course, you don't become *less* interested in playing the great courses. You want to go to Augusta. It becomes your dream." In other words, Vegas is the home of the Masters of gambling, but it's open to the public year-round.

The flip side of this trend is that gamblers who do go to Vegas don't want to see rug-rats everywhere. Customers were telling the casinos that they didn't like seeing crying babies in strollers going by the tables. The spread of gambling around the country has, for better or for worse, made Americans more serious about wagering. And, let's face it, everybody turns into [comedian] W.C. Fields at the blackjack table: "Get away from me, kid, you're bothering me."

A second reason so many women are taking off their clothes inside the casinos is that there are so many women taking off their clothes *outside* the casinos. Almost simultaneously with the explosion of gambling around the country, strip clubs have become a major business in the U.S. In Las Vegas, these joints have been shaving millions—more likely hundreds of millions, though nobody knows for sure—from the casino's coffers. "These guys leave the table at midnight to go get their lap-dances—and whatever else they can get, if you know what I mean," explains a blackjack dealer. "Oh, sure, I'm taking horny guys from the casinos to Club Paradise or the Palomino [strip clubs] all the time," a cabbie says. "You want me to take you there?"

When casinos hope to feed, house, clothe, and entertain their guests for the duration of their stay, an exodus of high-dollar patrons is a big deal. So, with this loss to their bottom lines in mind, the casinos have added lines of bottoms to their entertainment roster.

The last reason for the makeover is the simplest: Vegas decided to stop apologizing for what it is. The day-care centers, amusement parks, and Imax theaters are all great and they're here to stay. But let's face it: Vegas is about booze, sex, and gambling. Take away these things and you have a lot of hotel rooms in the desert. With the spread of gambling and generalized raunchiness around the country, the casinos concluded they could move away from the Disney-style wholesome goodness without losing any family travelers, or even generating much controversy.

Corporate "Sleaze"

But the funny thing is that the new Vegas "sleaze" is just as fake, or rather just as "corporate," as the goody-goody Vegas was. The make-believe sarcophagi at the Luxor or the medieval jousting at the Excalibur wasn't real, and neither is most of the "smut" at the big casinos. Oh, sure, they're real boobies (okay, not *completely* real), but the idea is to create an ambiance in which generally upright Americans can feel a bit naughty. After all, almost 60 percent of Vegas visitors are women. Just

as the van Goghs at the Bellagio offered a fig leaf of sophisti-
cation for vacationers a little embarrassed to be going to Las
Vegas—the equivalent of offering articles between the pictures
of *Playboy*—the new burlesque prunes that fig leaf back a little
bit, without getting rid of it. Now that Vegas is acceptable, it
can afford to be a little more saucy. But, in the end, it's still
smut as kitsch.

The Shadow Bar at Caesars Palace may be the most hyped
of the new sin-city attractions. Officially called "Shadow: A
Bar at Caesars Palace"—no doubt because colons make names
saucy—the gimmick centers on several dancers who prance
and gyrate behind a translucent screen that allows the patrons
at the bar to see only their silhouettes. Most of the dancers are
women, but there are also some men, who look especially silly.

Various travel writers have noted that the Shadow Bar
"epitomizes" the new "sin is in" culture of Las Vegas. But
when I was there, the crowd seemed virtually indistinguishable
from the sort of folks you see at a "Cheers" bar at the airport.
Indeed, just as the "Cheers" franchise lamely tries to capture
the feel of the bar and TV show it's named after, the Shadow
Bar seems to be going for an homage to the *Our Man Flint*
movies of the 1960s.

Big-casino Vegas isn't sleazy so much as it is a Sleaze Land
theme park. The really dirty strip clubs aren't scared of the
competition from shows like "Midnight Fantasy," which, the
Luxor insists, is "classy and tasteful." On any smut-o-meter,
such shows are like the kiddie-car rides at Disney World;
everyone knows that the more exciting "big-kid" go-karts can
be found elsewhere in Orlando. As a co-owner of the Spear-
mint Rhino, a popular strip club, explained to *USA Today*: "It's
the difference between watching the Playboy Channel and
having the Playboy girl come over and rub you down."

Indeed, if the crowd at "Midnight Fantasy" is any indica-
tion, the Playboy Channel version is saucy enough for now. As
I left the theater—as quickly as I could—I ran into a nice elderly couple. The gentleman said with a broad grin, "Boy, you
lucked out in there!" Before I could say anything in response,
his wife said, "Don't embarrass him. He probably doesn't want
anyone to know he's here."

You could say that again.

3

EXAMINING POP CULTURE

Games
People Play

Waterfront Casinos in Mississippi

Tim Stafford

While legalized gambling takes several forms in the United States including lotteries, video poker, and horse racing, casino gambling has arguably made the greatest impression on the popular culture and is typically what comes to mind when many people think about gambling. The image of a player rolling the dice at a craps table, spinning the roulette wheel, pulling the lever on a slot machine, or "doubling down" at blackjack has been repeated in countless Hollywood movies and television programs. Since 1988, casino gambling has spread from Nevada and New Jersey to a total of twenty-nine states, due in large measure to revenue-hungry state governments and the proliferation of Indian casinos. With more than eight hundred casinos now operating in the United States, the majority of Americans have tried their luck at casino games.

In the following essay, Tim Stafford describes how waterfront casinos—located on riverboats and floating barges—have become big business in Mississippi, one of the most religious and socially conservative regions of the country. Rather than seeing it as an immoral vice, many Mississippians increasingly view gambling as a fun, civic-minded activity that generates both jobs and state revenues. Stafford is a regular contributor to *Christianity Today* magazine, a conservative, evangelical publication.

■

Tim Stafford, "None Dare Call It Sin," *Christianity Today*, vol. 42, May 18, 1998, pp. 35–38. Copyright © 1998 by Timothy Stafford. Reproduced by permission.

NOT LONG AGO, GAMBLING WAS ILLEGAL ALMOST everywhere. In those days, America sent gamblers into the desert to pursue their dissolution. Las Vegas—"Sin City"—existed like a disease under quarantine, separated from the commonwealth by hundreds of miles of arid wilderness. If you went to Las Vegas, you didn't tell your mother; you didn't take the kids.

But not today. Without much fuss, Vegas has come near to us all. You can legally gamble in 48 states of the Union. Gambling has become normal, like the sale of beer at Safeway. Casinos offer childcare.

Nowhere is this transformation more obvious, nor more surprising, than in poor, conservative, Bible Belt Mississippi, which now trails only Nevada in square feet of casino gambling space. Since 1992, Mississippi has grown 30 thriving casinos producing nearly $2 billion annual gambling losses. These losses are, of course, the casinos' gain, and the government's, for gambling operations are taxed by state and local authorities there at a 12 percent rate.

A Deep Strangeness

I began my tour of gambling in Mississippi at its southernmost part. As I followed State Highway 49 toward the Gulf of Mexico, billboards advertising games of chance slowly proliferated in the piney woods, until I reached Gulfport and saw my first Deep South casino. Downtown Gulfport looks beat-up and gray, with plenty of vacant storefronts and pawn shops. But on the waterfront gleam the Copa Casino—a converted cruise ship—and the glittering Grand Casino Gulfport, both seemingly lowered from a spaceship.

Mississippi's Gaming Control Act states that Gulf Coast casinos must be floating in the gulf waters. The Grand Casino sits on a barge so vast it is unthinkable that even a tidal wave could rock it. It has its own landside parking garage, its own 400-room hotel. You can walk upstairs and down on the gambling barge, from one mirrored wall to another, with only a vague sense that there is any world outside. The decor is gaudy and bright: patterned carpets, fountains of multi-colored lights, mirrored walls and ceilings. The electronic bells of slot machines make hypnotic background music against the harsher rhythm of large tokens dashing into metal trays—the sound, literally, of money poured out.

I had forgotten the deep strangeness of the casino environment. Whether I visited Mississippi casinos late at night or at 9:00 in the morning, I always found plenty of people, black and white, old and young, male and female, dressed in sweatshirts and jeans and pantsuits—a Kmart crowd. Most play the slots. They sit holding plastic drink cups full of quarters, smoking, drinking, patiently tending the simple machines that roll ahead every ten seconds to inform them whether they have won or lost money. The atmosphere is surprisingly chaste. No cocktail waitresses approach in skimpy costumes. Clean and bright childcare facilities are available. Even when a slot machine is slamming out a reward, no excitement is visible—no whooping or hollering, no hugging or high fives. You would not readily imagine that this is entertainment. It has more the flavor of an assembly line.

And yet, the people are there, spending (losing) large amounts of money. They come from throughout the South— Georgia, Florida, Alabama and Texas, Louisiana, Tennessee, and Arkansas, to judge by the license plates in the parking lot. About a third of the gamblers are Mississippians, according to the casinos.

I crossed to the other side of the street in the morning, to the sober red brick of First Baptist Church. Pastor Kiely Young met me in worn cowboy boots. He told me he had fought hard against the casinos. "Unfortunately," he said, "our projections of negative impact have been fulfilled." The church's benevolence ministry—handouts and help to needy people—has tripled since the casinos arrived in 1992. One prominent church member recently made the front page of the local paper. He lost his law practice, his family, and his place in the community to gambling and drink he couldn't control. Young told me of another high roller who was met at the airport by a casino limousine. After he had lost everything—and since the casinos offer ATMs, and credit card advance losses can be much more than what you carry in your wallet—the same limo drove him to the Salvation Army.

Spectacular flops make the Mississippi newspapers—like the three children under five years old who, left in the parking lot while their parents played the slots, set the family car on fire and almost killed themselves. Or the elementary school teacher arrested for embezzling $1,800 in Adopt-a-School funds to feed her gambling habit. Or the father of two, over $100,000 in debt to a casino, who killed himself after losing the last $40 in his wallet. I found plenty of such stories in back issues of the newspapers, and I heard more from the pastors I visited. Pastors feel the burden of increased social dysfunctions—more marriage counseling, more people hitting the church office for financial help. Yet they almost visibly shrugged when I asked what the church can do about it. Gambling has come to Mississippi for good, they say, and the only role they see for themselves is picking up the pieces.

That's partly because of the enabling legislation. Mississippi's law allows individual counties along the Mississippi River and the Gulf Coast to vote on whether they want gambling. The catch is that if citizens vote no, gambling proponents can call for another election a year later—and keep calling them forever. (The "waiting period" has been lengthened for some counties.) If citizens vote yes, however, gambling is legalized forever. There's no way to reverse the choice.

Even if there were, it's very unlikely Gulfport and their near neighbors in Biloxi would do it. They love the money. "That's what put us on the map," Pastor Young said. "That's what stabilized the economy."

Thousands of new jobs have been created. Real estate prices are soaring. Housing subdivisions and huge hotels are under construction. Championship golf courses are in the making, causing people to hope the Mississippi coast might become a destination resort.

The casinos bring in name entertainers. Casinos offer attractive and inexpensive restaurants (I don't know how many people told me that you can get steak and lobster for $5.99) and burnish an image of Mississippi as a smart and savvy place.

Memphis magazine put it this way: "Mississippi lawmakers, regulators, and casino operators made decisions that were smarter, bolder, and ultimately more profitable than competitors'. . . . The skeptics who said 'the nation's fiftieth state' was too small, too conservative, too religious, too isolated . . . were wrong."

It is not lost on Mississippians—even Mississippi Baptists—that people in a big place like Memphis now admire their smarts, perhaps for the first time in history.

It remains to be seen whether the economic development has a wide impact. Casinos hire a lot of barmaids, but most of the jobs don't have a strong career path. Will the boom keep going, transforming the region, or will it leave a poor community with some gaudy casinos on its margins? The lessons of Atlantic City would favor the latter; Las Vegas, the former.

So far the beach strip shows few signs of renovation—it's still dominated by curio and T-shirt stores, aging motels, and graceful old homes. One of those homes is Beauvoir, the last home of Jefferson Davis, president of the Confederacy. I stopped to tour the well-preserved house, and strolled a sandy path to an old oak tree where an aging Davis would sit and read his Bible. I couldn't help wondering what old Jeff Davis would think of the casinos, visible just down the beach. He led a rebellion not just to preserve slavery, but to protect the South's traditional, agrarian way of life—a world ruled by concepts of honor and nobility. That's all gone now. Money rules Mississippi.

How the Legislation Passed

The Southern Baptists of Mississippi wield considerable influence, and if you doubt it, you should see the large office building they own across from the state capitol in Jackson. There I met Elizabeth Holmes and Paul Jones from the Baptist Christian Action Commission. When I asked them how it happened that Bible Belt Mississippi had accepted gambling casinos, Jones recalled a lunch he had with a very confident casino executive back in 1985.

Mississippi would surely become a gambling state, the executive had predicted, for three reasons. First, Mississippi was such a poor state, "the economic argument will be heard." (The campaign to bring gambling to the Gulf Coast used the slogan, "Vote Yes for Jobs.") Second, white Christians would fail to find allies against gambling among a new breed of black leadership, who remember too well the failure of white Christians to confront racism. Third, "Mississippi is probably as good an example of cultural Christianity as we have ever seen anywhere. We'll get the businessmen, and once we've got them, we'll silence the church."

That was the year, Jones explained, that the president pro tem of the state senate was caught taking a $50,000 bribe. His arrest and imprisonment set back gambling interests for several years. Then, in 1989, Governor Ray Mabus proposed a new educational agenda, seeking to fund it through the establishment of a lottery. Baptists and other antigambling forces fought and defeated the lottery bill. The next year, the governor called a special session of the legislature to consider again educational reform. It happened that Southern Baptists and Methodists were holding their annual meetings that week, so many pastors were out of town. When they returned home on Saturday, they learned that the legislature had established the Mississippi Gaming Commission. Two years later, in August 1992, the first casino opened its doors.

I went by the Gaming Commission, where a helpful public relations officer, Warren Strain, gave me detailed statistical information on the gambling industry and explained how the commission's oversight operates. "We're not for it and we're not against it," he stressed, "even though it does put bread on my table." Strain verified that the casino operations are at pains to show themselves clean and mob free.

I drove out to Vicksburg to visit one of the casinos built on the Mississippi River, stopping to see the Civil War battlefield on the way. The tourist slogan is, "History . . . and so much more." It appears that this means, "History . . . and gambling." Unfortunately, people who are interested in history don't much gamble, and vice versa. The town of Vicksburg looks as though it had died and someone forgot to bury the body. At the top of the famous bluff overlooking the Mississippi is the old town, with handsome spired churches and historic houses. At the bottom, on the river, is Harrah's casino, an ersatz neon riverboat. In between is an attempt to establish a street of boutique shopping, with brick sidewalks. Half the stores are empty. The riverboat no doubt brings tax money to Vicksburg, but it evidently does no more for its environment than a tire factory.

That's not necessarily an indictment, however. I tried to think how Vicksburg would be altered if the casinos became factories for some other useless product—bobble-head dolls, for instance. I'm sure Mississippi would happily accept regional leadership in bobble-head doll manufacturing. The jobs would require, presumably, about the same skill levels as do casino jobs. The main difference would be felt by the addicts. There are no problem consumers of bobble-head dolls the way there are problem gamblers. And the state, addicted to revenue, would never be able to tax a manufacturer at 12 percent of revenue. . . .

The Pornography of Success

Most Protestants have viewed gambling as inherently problematic, if not sinful (in point of fact, a lot of Christians—Catholics particularly—never have seen gambling as sin). Gambling may be entertainment, but it is not wholesome entertainment—it depends on lust as surely as does pornography. Gambling appeals to people's fantasies that they can get something for nothing. It is the pornography of success, undermining that important element of character known as the work ethic—the conviction that all people need to work persistently at productive tasks.

The vast majority of people can "handle it," as the gambling industry is quick to point out, but gambling does cause persistent social problems. Poor people tend to gamble away larger percentages of their income, so it's a "tax" on those who can't afford it. A recent study found that the poorest of Mississippians—those making less than $10,000 a year—spend more than 10 percent of their income on gambling if they live in a county where it's legal. Most troubling of all, a certain percentage of people—estimates run from 1.5 to 6.5 percent—can't control their gambling, and these "problem gamblers" increase when gambling is readily available. Problem gamblers become the embezzlers, bank robbers, suicides, child abusers, and bankrupts you read about in the newspaper. Robert Goodman in *The Luck Business* estimates that each "problem gambler" costs society $13,200 a year, including bankruptcies, fraud, embezzlement, unpaid debts, and criminal justice costs. Other estimates range from $20,000 to $30,000.

A 1997 study from Mississippi State University estimated there are between 46,400 and 88,700 problem gamblers in

Mississippi. If Goodman's estimates of social costs are accurate, then problem gamblers cost Mississippi at least $600 million annually—a lot more than casinos pay in taxes. However, the cost of problem gamblers is diffuse, while the taxes are money in the bank.

Really, the argument over gambling rarely reaches this level, because the rhetoric of choice sweeps every other argument away. For economic conservatives, casinos offer a pure form of capitalism: an ingenious product sold to willing buyers. Mississippi casinos promote economic development without much government involvement; they keep taxes low; and they locate only where local counties vote to invite them in. Isn't this what [conservative Republican] Newt Gingrich has been advocating—low taxes, less government, local control? The logic of the market won't let some higher authority say what products are worthwhile or restrain unwise choices by consumers. If people like to buy bobble-head dolls, let them. If they get a bigger kick out of pouring money into slot machines, that's their choice. If they blow away their rent money in the process—that's their problem, not mine.

The rhetoric of choice appeals to liberals, too, though in a different way. Liberals react against traditional moralism. Abortion, pornography, sexual behavior, saluting the flag—these they think should be a matter of choice, not public morality. (On other matters, of course, liberals can become quite moralistic.) Regarding gambling, why should the state tell people whether it's wrong? Why shouldn't people choose for themselves? Meanwhile, casinos satisfyingly integrate different ethnic groups (gambling is a great leveler) and offer jobs to poor people rather than lecturing them on their need to stay married and to avoid drugs and crime.

So both conservative and liberal impulses meet when gambling is legalized. It's probusiness yet socially liberal. Actually, you'll notice this combination on most of the social vices. Pornography, alcohol, gambling, tobacco—where would they be without corporate America? Vice makes excellent business, and businesses promote vice very efficiently. Only they don't call it vice. In America today we don't have any language to discriminate between legitimate and illegitimate business. As Warren Strain of the Mississippi Gaming Commission put it,

"We're not for it and we're not against it, even though it does put bread on my table."

Mardi Gras on the Mississippi Delta

The strangest locale for gambling is Tunica County. Located in the cotton fields of the Mississippi Delta, Tunica is two-thirds black and desperately poor—on some lists, the poorest county in America. At least it was until the casinos got in.

Most of the traffic into Tunica comes by way of Memphis, a mere 30 minutes' drive. I came the other direction from Jackson, following straight, narrow highways. I don't remember seeing a new building on the entire drive. I didn't see many old buildings, either—this part of the country is relatively unpopulated. The cotton was coming in, so all along the roads, head-high bricks of cotton waited to be ginned. Unpicked cotton laced the fields like an early snow. Then, through the hazy November afternoon I saw, from far off, the gleaming 30-story tower of the Lucky Strike Hotel, under construction.

There is no town nearby. Really, there is nothing nearby. The Tunica casinos don't sit on water but starkly alone on the river side of the Mississippi levee. The large, gaudy buildings are mostly built on a theme—Irish castle, Mardi Gras, Country, Hollywood, Wild West. Gamblers come from nearby Tennessee and Arkansas, though new golf courses and a 30-story hotel suggest that the casinos plan to reach out to a wider region. Already, the casinos offer more jobs than there are residents in the entire county. Welfare rolls are down, way down. Tax dollars have poured in faster than the local authorities know how to spend them. It's a stunning change for a place that hasn't seen much.

Yet the change is not uniform. I stopped in at the Baptist building in Clarksdale to talk to W.C. Johnson, the 70-year-old director of missions for Baptists in the North Delta. His threadbare office gives supplementary relief to people short on money, and they are having a banner year—more people showing up looking for help than ever before. Funds are short, Johnson said, since local Baptist offerings are down, as is church attendance. There are three pawnshops in Clarksdale where there used to be one, and two clothing stores recently went under. Johnson wanted to be fair, and he made a point to tell me that the casino money did a lot to improve roads and build new schools. The casinos, from what he hears, treat their employees with dignity and fairness. But, "These people who live in the Delta can't afford to gamble. Losing $50 for them is like $1,000 for someone else."

I asked him how pastors in the area feel about the casinos. He said that, black or white, local pastors oppose gambling, seeing the damage it does in families. They feel helpless to say much, though. "Most of them have decided that preaching is not going to work." One Baptist pastor wanted to take out an ad in the local paper, stating that his church would have nothing to do with the casinos. When he went to calculate how many families kept completely clear, however, he could come up with only a handful. He pulled the ad. Even people who don't gamble like to get a cheap meal at the casinos. "My son and his wife go a lot," Johnson said. "I asked him if he would grow a beard for my sake."

I ended my trip just over the state line in Memphis, where I visited relatives. My niece, a recent college graduate, told me that she frequently accompanies friends to Tunica for an evening of gambling. The rest of the family goes less often but consider it a lot of fun when they do. My brother-in-law, a doctor in a medical research lab, told me that his working group planned to take a bus to Tunica instead of holding a Christmas party. They had done it once before, and the feeling is strong that it was the best Christmas celebration they ever had. He theorized that people from very different social strata—doctors and lab technicians and secretaries—feel more comfortable together in a casino than they would at a party.

I thought I detected a slight uneasiness in the way they talked to me about it—as if to say, "Who would have ever imagined me enjoying a casino!" Yet it was evident that gambling had become a quite normal way for an educated, civic-minded family to have fun.

Memphis magazine reports that people in Memphis lose about $450 million annually to the Tunica casinos. According to a 1997 poll, they are split right down the middle—half visiting the casinos and half staying home, half thinking the casinos have made a positive impact and the other half considering it negative. Is there a debate going on, however? Not in the least. It's a free market, and if you don't like gambling, you don't have to go.

Most Americans don't have any moral language to talk about whether gambling is a good thing for us as a community. Commerce is the only language we hold in common, and it speaks of choice. I didn't know what to say, therefore, when my relatives told me how much they enjoyed gambling. What language could convince them that gambling is a sin?

Indian Casinos: Cultural Exchange and Gambling

Stephen Goode

Casinos run by Indian tribal governments on reservations became a major force behind the spread of casino gambling throughout the United States in the 1990s. In 1988, Congress passed the Indian Gaming Regulatory Act, which set the terms under which Indian tribes could broker agreements with states to run casinos on their lands, a right established by a 1987 Supreme Court ruling. Since many tribes are beset with high unemployment and widespread poverty, casinos were embraced as a way to address longstanding social problems. The result of these changes is that more than one-third of the five hundred recognized tribal governments in the United States now run casinos in twenty-nine states.

While not all Indian casinos have been profitable, some tribes, like the Mohegans and the Pequots in Connecticut, have turned casinos into successful, multibillion-dollar enterprises. In the following article, Stephen Goode describes a visit to the Mohegans' vast casino and hotel complex—Mohegan Sun—which opened in 1996 near the town of New London. According to the author, the Mohegans have incorporated tribal symbols and mythological imagery into the design of the complex to present their cultural heritage to gamblers. Tribal leaders

■

hope that gamblers will gain an appreciation for how casino profits have revived and sustained Mohegan culture. Goode is a senior staff writer for *Insight on the News*, a conservative current events magazine published by the *Washington Times*.

THE INVITATION WAS IRRESISTIBLE. "COME VISIT the Casino of the Sun," it said. Have fun. It promised a detailed and lingering tour of a vast new $1 billion complex whose architecture and decor would stun the eye, and it spoke alluringly of grand restaurants guaranteed to please even the most fastidious palate.

A Tribe's New Addition

It also promised "a legendary gaming experience" and entertainment of many kinds, all on the same spot: the Mohegan Sun, a vast complex that spreads across the landscape of eastern Connecticut along the Thames River, a few miles north of New London.

It all belongs to the Mohegan Indians—the same tribe that James Fenimore Cooper wrote about in *The Last of the Mohicans* and which he mistakenly thought was gone from the face of the Earth. In 1996, these American Indians opened the Casino of the Earth—180,000 square feet of gambling and entertainment space that is generating annual earnings of $700 million. In November 2001, the press was invited to witness the tribe's new addition, the Casino of the Sun, which increases that space to 315,000 square feet and offers a long list of other "gotta-visit" attractions: 22 new restaurants and retail outlets, in addition to the old section's 18, for a total of 40.

In April 2002, the Mohegan Sun's 34-story hotel opened. Mohegan officials say they expect the center's earnings to climb to $1 billion in one to two years, despite the recent economic downturn and the war on terrorism. They also predict that 3,500 new employees will be added to the already more than 10,000 now working at the center, making it a major employer in New England.

The Casino of the Sun's opening was low-key. Originally plans had been big time: "Pyrotechnics and much else," Mohegan Tribal Council Chairman Mark Brown tells [the author]. But the terrorist attacks of September 11, [2001] put the quietus on those plans. Officials opted for a ribbon-cutting ceremony along with a long moment of silence for those lost at the World Trade Center, the Pentagon and in Pennsylvania.

A large American flag hung during the short ceremony. Tribal elder Ernest Gilman—a career Navy man, now retired, whose Mohegan name is Kiwa—lit a small fire that sent a slender column of smoke into the air, chanted for a short time in what was said to be Mohegan and then translated: "Thanks be to the Creator. The Creator is good. Enjoy!"

Nothing Flashy

It was a short and sweet introduction to the vast new casino. [The author] has visited other Indian gaming places all over the United States, including Foxwoods, the Pequot tribe's humongous eastern Connecticut casino only 18 miles distant from the Mohegan tribe's undertaking. But the Mohegan Sun's invitation had promised something different from the standard gambling scene: a place intended for more than a center for gaming and good times, even though those are its prime purpose: a complex that in addition would convey what it means to be a Mohegan. And, to an amazing extent, it delivers on that promise.

Slot machines of course are everywhere—more than 6,000 of them—along with other games—blackjack, roulette, craps, baccarat, to name only a few. And most of the 40,000 or so souls at opening day appeared to be avidly engaged in making use of them all. What's different at the Mohegan Sun is that, first, the place is noticeably less gaudy than most casinos (though it assuredly glitters spectacularly) and, second, there's been a conscious, painstaking effort to weave the tribe's own history and mythology into the complex's art and architecture, right down to the smallest detail.

A casino short on gaudiness? Well, yes. It's one of the first things, for instance, that Sal (Mohegan employees wear name tags bearing their first names only), a 22-year veteran of the gambling business [mentions]. Sal says he helped "bring gambling to Atlantic City [N.J.]" then worked at gaming houses in New Orleans (which he didn't like because "folks there prefer drinking to gambling") and on the Gulf Coast. Sal is now a floor manager at Mohegan Sun. He quickly runs down casinos in Las Vegas. Why? "Because there's too many gaudy lights there. Not like here."

It's a sentiment shared by tribal elder Gilman. The Mohegan Sun is "nothing flashy," he insists to [the author]. "I wouldn't have it any other way." It's a matter of tribal pride. Gilman, now 67, is the grandnephew of the Mohegan tribe's most esteemed member and medicine woman—Gladys Tantaquidgeon, who was born in 1899 and now is 102. It's a relationship that has helped him keep his Mohegan origins always in mind. "I always knew who I was and where I came from," he says, even when his employer, the U.S. Navy, sent him far away. He's pleased with the Mohegan Sun because there's so much of the Mohegan "past in the place, so many things I know as a Mohegan."

Conveying Tribal Culture

The plans to make it all as Mohegan as possible were in gear from the beginning. Tribal leaders early on handed David Rockwell, head of Rockwell Architecture, and his associates a 300-page summary of Mohegan legends, art, crafts and oral history. "They grasped it so quickly," tribal leader Brown tells [the author]. "They think like we [Mohegans] do now."

It was a task that Rockwell and his designers were pleased to undertake. "It was a dream-come-true project," says the famous architect, simply because it wasn't just filling a big empty space with eye-catching dazzle. "It was a chance to convey the story, history and aspirations of a particular people, the Mohegans, in a dramatic way."

Bellagio, the Las Vegas casino, famously has $300 million worth of Picassos, Monets and Van Goghs [paintings] in its lobby to attract whatever culture-hungry gamblers may exist. The Mohegan Sun itself would become its own work of art, a kind of theme park of things Mohegan.

How to do this? For one thing the designers took symbols common to Mohegan baskets, belts and tribal regalia (such as a four-dome design and another called "the tree of life") and made ample use of them throughout the complex.

There are carefully beaded designs on ceilings, and in the

300-seat cabaret there are exquisite tiles that symbolize earth, wind, fire and water. "A huge group of craftsmen worked on the place," [explains] Edmond Bakos, one of Rockwell's assistants, a claim that's probably true. Almost everywhere one casts an eye there's been a great deal of effort expended on detail: burlap blended into plaster walls, for example, to create a rough texture, or glass beads in plaster to convey the feeling of the drying-up period after a storm in "Rain" one of the Casino of the Sun's several upscale restaurants.

The Mohegan tribe's traditional closeness to nature is a main theme. A huge canopy suggesting a turtle shell covers a gambling area for nonsmokers. In Mohegan mythology, the world took shape as a small group of islands on the back of a turtle standing in a giant pond. The Mohegans are known as the "wolf people" and, throughout the complex, stuffed wolves that look as live as they once were hover on ledges above casino patrons, their heads turning right and left, their tails twitching.

From Waterfalls to the Big Dipper

There's an 85-foot waterfall, too, which attracted the interest of Tom and Trudy Goodrow, residents of nearby Uncasville, Connecticut. They read about the falls and decided to come see it. The waterfall is named Taughannick Falls because on a tribal migration the Mohegans, according to legend, passed through the Taughannick Mountains "where there were many waterfalls." The Goodrows call themselves "recreational, five-or-six-times-a-year gamblers" and Tom, a retired industrial engineer, holds one of those large cups used to catch the winnings from the slots. They tell [the author] that they used to fly down to Atlantic City to gamble and are delighted that now there's a casino just next door.

The waterfall is eye-catching but, right in front of it, and at the halfway point between the older Casino of the Earth and the new Casino of the Sun, is what may be the single most extraordinary object in the whole Mohegan Sun—a 25-foot-tall, 14-foot-wide Dale Chihuly sculpture made of 2,500 sections of blue, clear and silver glass that seem to turn, twist and writhe even though they move not at all.

The sculpture weighs five tons and looks like the huge

splash that might have happened if a 10-ton boulder had slid over the Taughannick Falls. The Seattle-based Chihuly has become world famous for his work in glass, his chandeliers having created a whole new definition of what a chandelier can be. Not surprisingly, Chihuly's Mohegan Sun sculpture is a crowd-pleaser. Nine of the 10 people asked [by the author] what they thought of it didn't pause a second before replying, "Beautiful!" The 10th waited a moment, then said she liked it okay but added that exactly what it was remained a mystery to her. Mohegan officials won't say what they paid for it, but the price reportedly was something slightly more than $1 million.

Fittingly, the centerpiece of the Casino of the Sky is a huge planetarium. The domed ceiling shows the heavens as they were in May 1994, when the Mohegans celebrated their official federal recognition as a tribe. There's Orion and the Big Dipper and a huge full moon that travels across the sky. Hot-air balloons make the trip, too, in breathtaking groups of as many as five. And there's a jet plane that flies from one horizon to the other, followed by its vapor trail.

Directly under this big sky is Wombi Rock, three stories high and made of onyx. The words "Mohegan Sun" are a bilingual pun. Sun meaning the bright star nearest Earth in English, but in Mohegan "sun" means rock—and some kinds of rocks (quartz in particular, of which onyx is a variety) are sacred to the tribe. The onyx, brought from Pakistan, Iran and Mexico, was fused with glass in Italy, then brought to the United States and assembled on the spot into the large, hollow boulders that make up Wombi Rock.

Hypnotized Patrons

A gambling-free bar graces the top of Wombi. It offers a great view of the planetarium sky and a bird's-eye look at much of the Casino of the Sun. On each table is a menu listing 53 varieties of martinis. Plush, overstuffed easy chairs allow guests to stare at the moon and stars, which is exactly what John and Carol Brokaw of Ocala, Florida, are doing—hypnotized, like most everyone else in the bar, by the ongoing display.

John, who works for Flack & Kurtz Inc., is an engineer who helped plan the casino's plumbing. In a month, he'll go on to another job in Chicago. Neither he nor Carol are gamblers, but they love to just look, and Carol likes to shop. "Why watch my money disappear into a slot machine when I can buy something real," she says with a laugh.

One can visit stores here as varied as Boccelli (handbags), Godiva Chocolatier and The Golf Shop, each of which Carol had investigated that day. There's also Nostalgia, which specializes in 1940s and 1950s memorabilia and was very popular on opening day as fiftyish and sixtyish couples jitterbugged there to golden oldies introduced by a local disc jockey in a gold-lamé tux jacket.

At one of the shops that specializes in American Indian items, visitors can purchase a small book, *The Lasting of the Mohegans*. Published in 1995 before the opening of the first casino, it discusses at two or three places how "non-Indian money was . . . disdained by traditional Mohegans" and how some Mohegans centuries ago "embraced Christianity due to its espousal of anti-money philosophies," points-of-view that seem to be the author's editorializing and directly at odds with the existence of the hugely profitable Mohegan Sun. But some few Mohegans—including tribal chairman Brown's own brother—were cautious about the tribe opening a casino. What changed minds (or so most Mohegans will tell you) was what money could do to revive Mohegan culture and language and sustain the tribe's members.

Mostly a Crowd Pleaser

A very few first-day visitors to the Casino of the Sun weren't terribly impressed and said so. A Chinese-American businessman from New York City who is eating at Joseph White's Summer Shack, a casino eatery specializing in seafood, tells this writer and *Insight* photographer Rick Kozak, "You guys should get to A.C." This confuses us at first until it dawns on us that "A.C." is Atlantic City, whose atmosphere he most definitely prefers.

But mostly this crowd likes the Mohegan Sun and likes it a lot. A shy elderly lady who takes me for a casino employee walks past without stopping. "You people have it over all the other casinos," she says with a big grin.

Julia Mason, an African-American from New York City, came on a bus for the opening. She's a bit disgruntled because the trip was a long one with police stopping trucks in the aftermath of the attacks on the World Trade Center. She's standing by the Chihuly sculpture and claims she'd like to dismantle the sculpture and take it home with her. It's a big thing, she says, but she likes it a lot and she'd find a place for it. "I love it," she says. How does she like the whole place? The new Casino of the Sun and the older Casino of the Earth? "Donald Trump, eat your heart out!" she replies, and turns back to look at the sculpture.

Sports Betting: The American Pastime

Richard O. Davies and Richard G. Abram

Each year American sports fans wager hundreds of billions of dollars on college and professional sporting events with illegal bookies, the sports betting section of Nevada casinos, and in office pools. Every morning, sports bettors consult the numerous television and radio programs, daily newspapers, and Internet services that provide national betting lines and tips to give them an edge on upcoming games. In the following selection, Richard O. Davies and Richard G. Abram, the authors of *Betting the Line: Sports Wagering in American Life*, maintain that sports betting intensifies the interest and viewing pleasure of fans and is the driving force behind the enormous popularity of sports in the United States. Fears of game fixing, however, have led authorities to ban sports betting in every state but Nevada. The authors argue that since legalized gambling has spread to forty-eight states, lawmakers are wrong to continue their resistance to sports betting and are missing out on billions of dollars in tax revenue.

THE HISTORIAN JOHN FINDLAY GOT IT RIGHT when he identified Americans as a "people of chance." "From the seventeenth century through the twentieth," he writes, "both gambling and [the westward movement] thrived on high

■

expectations, risk taking, opportunism, and movement, and both activities helped to shape a distinctive culture." Despite the dim views taken of gambling within certain religious and social reform circles, it has been an integral and often unappreciated force in the development of American life and popular culture. American capitalism thrived on speculation, risk taking, and shrewd calculations of an investment's potential, but when these same traits were displayed at the racetrack or card table, many moralists were quick to condemn gamblers as slick thieves whose success made a mockery of such important values as the work ethic, thrift, and caution. As the historian Ann Fabian explains, a profound "moral confusion has plagued the whole long history of gambling in the United States."

Debate over Sports Betting

Although ambiguity about its role remains in some sectors of American society, gambling has overcome its once sinister image and the staunch opposition of antigambling organizations to become an integral part of the popular culture. By the end of the twentieth century major forms of gambling existed in forty-eight of the fifty states; only Hawaii and Utah did not offer some form of legally sanctioned gambling. Gambling is undoubtedly the biggest single industry in the United States, in terms of both revenues generated and the number of customers/participants. In the year 2000 an estimated 125 million Americans gambled at least once, putting some $2 trillion dollars into play. In 1999 even the resolute majority of social conservatives on the congressionally mandated National Gambling Impact Study Commission understood that prohibition or repeal of mainstream gambling was no longer politically feasible. They recognized that they had to content themselves with nibbling around the margins. "Once exotic, gambling has quickly taken its place in mainstream culture," the commission explained. "Televised megabucks drawings; senior citizens day trips to nearby casinos; and the transformation of Las Vegas into family friendly theme resorts, in which gambling is but one of a menu of attractions, have become familiar backdrops to daily life."

Although gambling has become an accepted part of everyday American life, the "moral confusion" that Fabian describes nonetheless remains, and it is especially evident in the continuing and contentious debate over the issue of sports betting. No one knows for certain how many Americans bet on sports, but it is estimated that about 25 percent of adult Americans make at least one bet on a sporting event each year—often by participating in modest office pools on the NCAA [National Collegiate Athletic Association] basketball tournament or the Super Bowl—while an estimated 15 million persons bet regularly and often heavily on football, baseball, basketball, prizefights, and horse races. Legal horse racing exists in thirty states, but other sports wagering is illegal in forty-nine of the fifty states. In the year 2000 only the maverick state of Nevada offered a full range of legal gambling opportunities on sporting events.

Horse racing, long a popular part of state tax collectors' portfolios, remains an important but slowly declining pastime for an aging group of dedicated horse players. Wagering on human sports, however, has become the primary focus of a new generation of sports gamblers. . . . Although sports wagering has grown from an estimated $20 billion wagered in 1975 to an estimated $80 billion in 1990, and upward to $200 billion in the year 2000, lawmakers in state capitals have been exceedingly reluctant to cut themselves in for a piece of the sports gambling action, although they have not hesitated to do so with pari-mutuel horse racing, million-dollar lotteries, bingo parlors, card rooms, and riverboat casinos.

The Driving Force Behind Sports

The reasons for this anomaly are deeply embedded in the nation's past. Sports wagering has long existed in the subterranean corridors of American life—illegal, condemned by reformers and concerned sports officials, but popular with substantial segments of the male population. Bookmakers have plied their illegal trade in urban places since the middle of the nineteenth century, making their peace with law enforcement and political bosses through a wide range of creative financial incentives. Although from time to time zealous reformers instigated crackdowns, the reform impulse would inevitably fade, and the bookmakers and their faithful clients would resume business as usual. By the late twentieth century, sports gambling had become so much a part of American life that it was generally ignored by law enforcement authorities. Sports gambling is and will undoubtedly remain for the foreseeable future one of the largest untapped sources of potential tax revenue in the nation.

Wagering is an important part of—some would say the driving force behind—the enormous popularity of sports in contemporary American society. It comes in many and often seemingly innocent forms: the five-dollar office pool on the NCAA basketball tournament or the World Series, a two-dollar Nassau bet among friends on the golf course, the weekly meeting of the Fantasy Football League, a casual day at the aging country fairgrounds watching the pacers and trotters go around the timeless oval, putting ten bucks down on a six-team college football parlay card with the bartender at the neighborhood tavern, or even making a twenty-dollar futures bet on the distant Super Bowl while visiting family-friendly Las Vegas during summer vacation.

Despite its central role in the growth of sports in twentieth-century America, gambling has been treated casually, if not with downright indifference by most sports historians. The reluctance of historians to delve into the complex topic of sports gambling—and sports history more generally—is readily understandable. For one thing, sports are often looked down upon by university faculty members as unnecessary and even corrupt appendages to the American system of higher education. Not interested themselves in team sports, and perhaps engaging in a bit of academic snobbery, they certainly do not want to make sports a part of their professional work. We find it intriguing that social historians, who have so often proclaimed their appreciation of the lives led by average citizens—the noble "common people"—have so overwhelmingly refused to examine the significance of sports history.

No society has ever evidenced such a level of interest in sports as the United States. Certainly, there is no society in the history of mankind in which sports have generated larger amounts of revenue. Yet, with a few exceptions, social historians have refused to incorporate into their classes and writings a subject in which ordinary Americans are deeply involved. It is our contention that, beyond the rather narrow realm of sports history, gambling on athletic contests holds much broader significance for the student of American history and popular culture, providing powerful insights into such larger issues a gender roles, class structure, ethnicity, modernization, local and national politics, and economic enterprise. At the very least, the subject deserves a larger place in the discourse of the rapidly increasing number of academic historians of sports. . . .

A Brief History of Sports Gambling

John Findlay's [author of the 1986 book *People of Chance*] pioneering study of gambling in the United States emphasized the formative role of the frontier and the American West. Although some forms of sports gambling can be traced to the colonial era and to the western frontier of the nineteenth century, the roots of modern sports gambling are to be found largely in the industrial cities of the post–Civil War period. Sports wagering in the United States has been and remains essentially an urban phenomenon. It is our contention, however, that sports wagering took on a distinctly new form in the years immediately following the Second World War. Like many other aspects of American life—such as civil rights, the economy, feminism, suburban life, communications, public education, mass entertainment—the structure of organized sports was fundamentally transformed by the powerful and galvanizing forces unleashed by the Second World War. Not only did organized sports in America grow exponentially in size and scope in the postwar era, but they were also fundamentally altered by new social and economic forces, including increased leisure time, a large increase in disposable income, changing demographic patterns that extended professional leagues to all points of the national compass, and fundamental changes in public values that came to view commercialized gaming as an acceptable form of leisure activity.

Television and Sports Betting

Television, however, was the primary force propelling sports wagering into a multibillion dollar industry during the latter half of the twentieth century. During the 1950s, network television programming created a much larger sports-viewing audience, generating high ratings for its coverage of baseball, football, basketball, and boxing. Television became, in a very real sense, an electronic form of *The Racing Form*, providing gamblers with enormous amounts of information regarding future wagers. Many sports fans discovered that if they had a bet down on a game being shown on television their viewing pleasure was intensified. The rapid expansion of cable television in the early 1980s produced a seemingly insatiable demand for sports programming, which in turn stimulated additional interest in sports betting.

The growth of organized sports during the age of television has been staggering. Major League Baseball, constricted to the northeastern quadrant of the nation and just eleven cities in 1950, grew to thirty teams by century's end. The National Hockey League is no longer the small private bailiwick of a handful of Canadian and northern American cities; the league now has franchises in such unlikely sunbelt cities as Miami, Dallas, Tampa–St. Petersburg, Nashville, Charlotte, Phoenix, and Los Angeles. But the greatest professional sports success story has been the National Football League [NFL], growing from a struggling eight-team league in 1945 to the thirty-two franchise multibillion dollar dynamo of today. In terms of fan interest and television ratings, it is now the unrivaled American game.

The NFL has become the intense focus of a new and more sophisticated generation of sports gamblers who for six months of the year closely follow the ebb and flow of computer-generated national betting lines published in daily newspapers, tune into an endless parade of radio talk shows that seek to provide a "bettor's edge" on upcoming games, watch cable television shows devoted exclusively to football handicapping, and subscribe to Internet tout services that sell their "releases" to an estimated two million subscribers each week. Nonetheless, professional football authorities will never publicly admit the obvious: that one of the most powerful forces propelling their product to the heights of fan popularity is that professional football offers an ideal format for sports wagering.

Millions Wagered on College Sports

College sports also benefited financially from this technological and commercial revolution. Where college football teams played nine-game seasons in 1950 with only a lucky handful of teams being invited to New Year's Day bowl games, by the year 2000 Division I-A teams routinely played eleven-game schedules—and sometimes an extra twelfth game thanks to preseason kickoff games, postseason conference playoffs, and trips to Hawaii—and twenty-five postseason bowl games. Division I-A college teams now play seasons that begin in early August with three weeks of preseason practice and do not end until five months later. Incredibly, the college football season starts weeks before the fall semester begins and ends after final exams are completed. Nearly all of these games are televised, either by one of several competing networks or by local stations, and thanks to the efforts of Nevada sports books, the national media, and an estimated 250,000 hustling illegal bookies in the other forty-nine states, they are the vehicle whereby untold hundreds of millions of dollars change hands between gamblers and bookmakers each week. College football coaches, a beleaguered if well-paid group of professionals, are often given to lamenting that, because of the popularity of betting by alumni and boosters, they are expected not only to win games but to beat the point spread in the process.

College basketball has been similarly influenced by television and the intense interest of gamblers. The introduction of the point spread idea at the end of the Second World War fundamentally changed the way in which gamblers bet on college basketball games: instead of taking odds on one team, they now bet on the number of points separating the two teams at the final buzzer. Introduction of the point spread in the mid-1940s had the effect of making every game a handicapping challenge to the gambler; it also created major problems for college officials. Some players, eager to earn spending money, became vulnerable to gamblers who, seeking a sure thing, offered them a modest payoff in return for winning a game by a margin less than the betting point spread. Because a basketball game, with only five players per team and a more unstructured form of play, is much less complex than football, it became the game of choice for unscrupulous gamblers/fixers during the postwar era. The point spread idea greatly increased the potential for fixed games.

The most famous fix of all occurred in 1919 when eight

members of the Chicago White Sox lost the World Series to the underdog Cincinnati Reds for a payoff of about $10,000 each. However, athletes on the take had been a significant, if largely ignored, part of the American sports scene long before the Black Sox Scandal, and they haven't disappeared yet. For the next eighty years gambling became the bane of professional and college sports officials as nasty headlines repeatedly proclaimed the latest scandal. Although many antigambling safeguards have been put in place, it seems that unscrupulous gamblers seeking the sure thing have found ways to circumvent the best preventative measures.

Singled Out

Fear of such misdeeds has caused sports gambling, of all the gambling venues, to be singled out for special treatment. In 2000 sports gambling was theoretically legal in four states—Nevada, South Dakota, New Jersey, and Oregon—but in reality it existed only in Nevada. Although it has been legal in the Silver State since 1931, sports wagering didn't become an important part of the Nevada casino scene until the 1980s, as a result of changed federal tax laws and the increased popularity of college and professional sports. In 1999 the National Gambling Impact Study Commission, a nine-person federal commission created in response to strong antigambling pressure from the socially conservative political establishment, disappointed its fervent supporters by submitting a bland and relatively benign final report that essentially suggested there were both good and bad features to the recently developed national gambling culture of state lotteries, Indian casinos, state-licensed casinos, riverboat casinos, and the proliferation of video poker and slot machines in several states. Only one form of gambling was singled out by the commission for criticism: legalized sports gambling in the state of Nevada. The commission's recommendation to make wagering on college games illegal nationwide was in part a response to the lobbying efforts of the National Collegiate Athletic Association, but in a broader context it was based upon a widespread uneasiness among the general public regarding sports gambling. The irony of this development is that sports wagering in Nevada's legal books [the part of the casino that accepts bets on athletic events] is the only casino gaming venue in which management does not have a built-in statistical advantage over the customer. Sports books can and do lose money, although the general ignorance of the betting public and the vagaries of Lady Luck have given the Nevada books a reasonable 4 percent take (before overhead) for the last twenty years. In 1999 the state's seventy-five sports books cleared a profit of about $100 million out of $2.5 billion wagered—small potatoes in the larger scheme of things for the bottom line–conscious corporate casino establishment that now controls Nevada's casinos.

Lottomania in North America

Chris Gudgeon and Barbara Stewart

Lotteries are games of chance in which participants purchase numbered tickets with the hope of winning cash or prizes. A popular means of raising money for schools and other projects in America until the late 1800s, lotteries were banned by every state in the union after high-profile scandals turned public opinion against them. In 1964, cash-strapped New Hampshire became the first state government to reintroduce a lottery and, based on its success, was soon followed by several other states. In 2003, thirty-seven states and the District of Columbia ran lotteries, and Americans spend billions of dollars on tickets each year. Chris Gudgeon and Barbara Stewart are the authors of *Luck of the Draw: True-Life Tales of Lottery Winners and Losers*. In the following excerpt from their book, the authors describe how a multistate, multibillion-dollar lottery jackpot during the summer of 1998 captured the public's imagination and prompted thousands of North Americans to wait in line for hours for their chance to become instant millionaires. This episode of lottery frenzy demonstrates how lotteries have grown into an indelible feature of American popular culture. Gudgeon is the author of nine books including *Consider the Fish* and *You're Not as Good as You Think You Are*. Stewart is the author of *Bloodlines: The Little Book of Vampires*.

■

Chris Gudgeon and Barbara Stewart, *Luck of the Draw: True Life Tales of Lottery Winners and Losers*. Vancouver: Arsenal Pulp Press, 2001. Copyright © 2001 by Chris Gudgeon and Barbara Stewart. Reproduced by permission.

MONEY. GOBS OF IT. EVERYONE DREAMS ABOUT it—almost no one can ever get enough of it. It doesn't grow on trees—surely your mother told you that—but sometimes, if you're lucky, it appears as if by magic. . . .

Instant Millions

The magic of the lottery, that is, which in an instant can transform a legal secretary or unemployed father or dock worker or waitress or bank manager into a multimillionaire. The lottery is the only reliable miracle left in this age of reason; no matter what else happens this week, you can be sure that someone, somewhere, will win it big.

It's an international obsession. Each week in North America alone, we spend almost half a billion dollars on lotteries and other state-run gambling schemes. Every year, seven out of ten adults buy at least one lottery ticket, while every state and province in North America runs at least half a dozen lottery schemes, from lotto draws to scratch-and-wins, to bingo games and, increasingly, casinos. Pretty remarkable considering that thirty years ago lotteries were illegal and held in contempt by upright people. Such "numbers games," it was said, were the domain of organized criminals, who preyed on the gullible and disadvantaged.

But beneath our lottery fantasies lurk nagging doubts about the personal, emotional, and social costs. "I'd hate to win a million," a cab driver in Montreal told us. "You lose your friends, your family, and you'd be afraid to walk the streets for fear someone would kill you just for your wallet." Despite his concerns, though, he shrugged and admitted that he never missed a draw. . . .

Lining up for Powerball

Maybe it was the heat. Something was certainly in the air the summer of 1998.

At first, there seemed to be nothing more than the usual interest in Des Moines–based Multi-State Lottery Association's [MUSL] July 29 Powerball draw. Less than a week before, the jackpot had flirted with the $100 million mark, but ticket sales were off some thirty percent and the hype didn't come close to the frenzy that preceded the May 20 draw, when people lined up for hours on a chance for a record $195 million prize pool.

Perhaps there was a prevailing sense of lunchbag letdown. The week following the record win, the jackpot reached a mere $10 million. Powerball sales declined dramatically, and no one seemed to care when the draw came and went without a winner. Could it be that in a country inundated with media messages—where 80 percent of the adult population gambled at least once in a while, and where lotteries alone were a $40 billion business—a $200 million jackpot just didn't grab the public's attention any more? The MUSL, an amalgamation of twenty states and the District of Columbia, had seen sales lulls before. But as draw after draw passed without a winner—nineteen in all—lottery organizers watched the prize pool grow without sparking the kind of lotto-buying lunacy they'd come to expect.

But all at once something clicked and it seemed that everyone caught the fever. Three-hour line-ups were the norm at many of the 45,000 ticket outlets, and in towns that bordered

---

Have I Got a Deal for You . . .

After their win, the Lucky 13 were inundated with once-in-a-lifetime opportunities. Like the TV producer who wanted to do a movie-of-the-week about the win; all he needed was a few million dollars to cover the cost of production. Or the songwriter who was working on a ballad about the lotto heroes; all he needed was a few thousand dollars to finish it. One guy even asked for $400,000 to develop his radiator repair business, $50,000 of which he promised to kick back to the groups' lawyer if the deal went through. There was also the usual collection of hard luck pleas for money, along with dozens of marriage and even indecent proposals. So far, the Lucky 13 have turned aside all offers.

Chris Gudgeon and Barbara Stewart, *Luck of the Draw: True-Life Tales of Lottery Winners and Losers*. Vancouver: Arsenal Pulp Press, 2001.

---

states that weren't part of the MUSL, some line-ups were running ten hours or longer. Extra police and security guards were brought in to keep the peace, while the urban myth machine worked overtime: a woman in Arizona, it was said, gave birth to twins as she waited in line to buy $200 worth of tickets; an elderly man in Greenwich, Connecticut—because of its close proximity to New York City, scene of some of the longest line-ups in the country—died waiting for his chance, his wife refusing to leave the queue until her husband's last act had been fulfilled.

Meanwhile, at Canada-U.S. border crossings, traffic was backed up for miles as those crazy Canucks, members of perhaps the most lotto-mad nation on earth, made pilgrimages to the nearest Powerball mecca. Powerball had a special power for Canadians: by the day of the draw, the jackpot had risen to almost $300 million, which when converted, worked out to almost $450 million Canadian. That's a lot of back bacon and beer.

As the July 29 draw deadline neared it was clear that it wasn't just the summer's heat driving people crazy: the lure of winning the big one had taken over. In four days, North Americans bought 150 million Powerball tickets, at a rate of 20,000 tickets a minute in the waning hours of the frenzy. One retailer in Connecticut reported selling more than 25,000 tickets a day, more—much more—than they'd expect to sell in a single week. And their take for all that hard work? At five cents per ticket, it worked out to $1,250—nothing to sneeze at, but hardly worth all the headaches. In fact, most vendors look at lottery tickets as a kind of loss leader, a high-maintenance low-profit item that helps to bring customers in the doors. There can be a silver lining, though; the store that sold the winning ticket was in line for its own windfall: a $100,000 bonus from the good folks at MUSL.

Finally, the moment of truth had arrived. At exactly 9:52 on Wednesday evening, the computerized ticket dispensers shut down. Although the final tally wouldn't be in for another day, the final sales total stood at $295.7 million. While it wasn't the world record the PR [public relations] people at MUSL claimed—Spain's famous El Gordo lottery regularly tops the billion-dollar mark—it was a healthy chunk of change and the biggest prize pool American lottery players had ever seen. With the draw only minutes away, the country held its collective breath.

The Roots of Powerball

What was this strange game and how did it come to outdraw almost every other lottery on the planet? The roots of Powerball go back to September 1987, when five states banded together to form the Multi-State Lottery Company. Overshadowed by more lucrative jackpots offered by big states like California and New York, the members of MUSL—Iowa, Kansas, Oregon, Rhode Island, and West Virginia, along with the District of Columbia—hoped to find strength, or at least safety, in numbers. Within the month, Missouri jumped on board and the MUSL was ready to launch its first game. It was called Lotto America, probably because a lot o' America couldn't have cared less about it: in its first six months, Lotto America had sales of around $32 million, chump change when you consider that the profits had to be split seven ways.

The following year, MUSL upped the ante, switching from a 7/40 style game (where winners had to pick seven correct numbers from one to 40) to a 6/54 game (six correct numbers out of 54). This made the game a little harder to win but also meant that the average jackpot would be bigger, and in the lottery game nothing succeeds like excess. Big jackpots mean big sales. The strategy was moderately successful, and by 1991 MUSL was enjoying annual sales of more than $400 million. But by now Wisconsin, Montana, Idaho, Indiana, Delaware, Kentucky, South Dakota, Maine, and Minnesota had joined in. There were a lot more potential players, but overhead was up accordingly as each member state's percentage split was down: the average take was under $12 million per state.

Still, MUSL had learned its lesson; players wanted low stakes games with big payoffs. In April 1992, the state-run corporation introduced its new baby: Powerball. In the beginning, it was a 5/45 + 1/45 game, meaning that winners had to pick five correct numbers out of a pool of 45 as well as one "powerball" number out of a pool of 45. Odds were listed at 55 million-to-one. Predictably, jackpots and sales increased, but after three years of record-breaking sales, Powerball took a U-turn south. Sales in 1997 reached just under $900 million, a drop of $300 million from the previous year. Part of the problem was that the state of Georgia, which had joined the lotto union in 1995, decided to drop out on moral grounds. The strong fundamentalist movement had persuaded the state legislature that lotteries were no way for a state to earn a living. But Powerball was also facing stiffer competition from other state lotteries as well as a range of other legal gambling options—from casinos to video lottery terminals to sports betting—which were starting to emerge. On top of everything else, five more states—Nebraska, Louisiana, Connecticut, New Hampshire, and New Mexico—had joined MUSL, which meant a further split of the profit. Something had to give.

That something came in the form of a kinder but not gentler Powerball. Launched in November 1997, the new game now featured a 5/49 + 1/42 format. The changes seem slight, but looks can be deceiving. The first part is relatively easy: the odds of getting five out of 49 numbers are a mere 1,906,684 to one, on a par with your chance of being killed falling out of bed. It's that damn red powerball that causes all the trouble; increasing the odds 42 times to a rather startling 80,089,128 to one; much better than your chance of being killed by a falling meteor, but significantly worse—42 times worse, in fact—than the odds of being struck by lightning. Ouch. Again, the strategy was to build up the prize pool. Officials from MUSL confidently predicted that within the year they'd see a $100 million jackpot; in fact, they had two in the first two months. Annual sales jumped back over the 1 billion mark and have stayed there ever since.

Lucky 13

At 10:59 P.M. on Wednesday, July 29 [1998], the two Beietel Criterion drawing machines at the MUSL's Des Moines headquarters whirled into action. One by one in numeric order, a lottery official fed 49 white high-density rubber balls, each slightly bigger than a golf ball, into one of the machines; the process was repeated in the other machine with 42 red Powerballs. The balls bounced around the drum for five seconds, then as the process slowed down, a hole opened up in the bottom of one drum. The lottery machine spat out the first white ball: number 43. Four more balls followed in quick succession:

8, 39, 45, 49. A moment later, the official opened the release at the bottom of the second machine. There was a pause before the ball rolled out: lucky number 13.

As the numbers were read out and transmitted to broadcast outlets across the country, you could almost feel the ground shift with the collective weight of several hundred million fallen expectations. Still, there were a lot of happy players. By design, Powerball combines two kinds of lottery games, which helps to spread the winnings around. On the one hand, Powerball offers a jackpot game, where a portion of all the money bet—roughly 29 percent—goes to a cash prize for people holding all six winning numbers. Meanwhile, there's also a set cash prize of $100,000 for anyone holding all five numbers on the 5/49 portion of the game, not to mention a three-dollar tip for anyone getting the right Powerball number. That means that, theoretically at least, there's no limit to the amount of money the MUSL could pay out in any given lottery. While statistically, the MUSL could expect to pony up ten $100,000 prizes each draw, that number frequently goes much higher. On July 29, when all was said and done, 79 players were five-ball winners, and another three million players had tripled their original one-dollar investment. And somewhere, someone or some group of someones held the single winning lottery ticket.

One of the people not watching the draw that night was John Jarrell of Parkridge, just outside of Columbus, Ohio. Convinced that the odds were not on his side, Jarrell had gone to bed, leaving a pile of Powerball tickets with his wife. For six years, Jarrell and his co-workers at Automation Tooling Systems in nearby Westerville had been pooling their money to buy tickets on the state lottery and every once in a while, when a big jackpot came along, they'd take a chance on that too. The giant Powerball jackpot was irresistible. Everyone in their group chipped in ten dollars to buy 130 tickets. John almost balked; things were tight, and ten bucks was twice what he already put out each week on the Ohio lottery. But finally, he joined in. A couple guys jumped in the car and drove to their favourite Powerball outlet, Speedway, 100 miles away in Richmond, Indiana.

Jarrell's wife Sandy watched the live broadcast of the Powerball draw, writing the numbers on a piece of paper. Then she compared the list with a stack of photocopied tickets. All of a sudden, her heart jumped. She ran to the bedroom, screaming for her husband to turn on the light.

He looked at the numbers. "We've got it," he told his wife. He waved the winning ticket—his ticket—to the biggest lottery jackpot in American history. [In May 2000, two ticket holders split a $363 million jackpot in Michigan. And in April 1999, Maria Grasso took home $197 million—the biggest unshared lottery pot in history.]

One Lump or 25?

The Jarrell's spent the rest of the night on the phone calling co-workers, friends, and relatives. By morning, they had a plan. They left the ticket in a safety deposit box—because it had to be redeemed in the state where it was bought, the ticket would later make the journey back to Indiana by armoured car—and John Jarrell met up with his 12 co-winners at work the next day. It was pandemonium: everyone was hugging and laughing and crying and giving high fives and slapping each other on the back. Even Robert Kronk was happy. Kronk wasn't one of the lucky thirteen, but if it hadn't been for a strange quirk of fate it could have been a different story. Kronk had been part of the lottery pool for years, but three months before the big draw he decided to drop out. He was tired of playing the quick pick—letting the computer select a random set of numbers—and wanted to take matters into his own hands. Big mistake.

At the end of the day, all that was left was for Jarrell and his partners to collect their winnings. But it wasn't as simple as that. First they had to decide: one lump or 25? See, Powerball gave them the option of taking the full jackpot amount in 25 equal annual payments or a one-time, lump sum buyout. These buyouts were always much less than the advertised jackpots, but in the long run, if properly invested, could prove much more lucrative. Ultimately, the Lucky 13 opted for a $161.5 million buyout which meant that, after taxes, each partner would take home roughly $6.8 million. And even though that figure was a far cry from the $297.5 million dreams of Powerball's frenzied fans, it did nothing to dim the success of the Summer of Lottery Love. It was perhaps the lottery's finest moment in this country, and proof that the luck of the draw had taken hold of our collective consciousness.

The Decline of Charity Bingo

Sarah Schweitzer

Bingo originated in America as a carnival game called "beano," which was based on a sixteenth-century Italian lottery game. New York toy salesman Edwin Lowe retooled the game to resemble its modern incarnation. Players try to match numbered squares on cards with numbers drawn at random by the bingo announcer. Since the early 1930s, American churches, synagogues, and charities have held weekly bingo games as a way to supplement the contributions of congregants and donors. Because of its popularity with churchgoers, bingo was the first form of gambling to be legalized in many states and has long served as a social outlet for its primarily elderly players. In the following article, *Boston Globe* reporter Sarah Schweitzer describes how church and charity bingo games are in decline, losing players to rapidly proliferating casinos where the games are faster and the prizes much higher. According to some observers, waning interest in charity bingo is weakening the social networks and sense of community that the games fostered.

THE LADIES STILL GATHER THURSDAYS AT THE Nazzaro Center, daubers primed and tales from the neighborhood ready for the telling. But it's not what it once was.

"We've lost a lot of people," said Rose Toscano, head of the Young Seniors weekly bingo game in Boston's North End.

■

Sarah Schweitzer, "Casino Bingo Cuts into Charity Share," *Boston Globe*, August 11, 2002, p. B1. Copyright © 2002 by Globe Newspaper Company. Reproduced by permission of the publisher, conveyed through Copyright Clearance Center, Inc.

In Search of Bigger Payouts

In some cases, the departures were unavoidable: "Death, Alzheimer's, and illness," as Toscano put it. But other players have drifted away, lured by the flashier, more lucrative bingo games at Foxwoods Resort & Casino [Indian casino near North Stonington, Connecticut] where payouts can reach $250,000. Bingo, the Plain Jane of the gambling world, long the province of coffee-sipping grandmothers eager for sociability as much as prizes, is poised to disappear from churches, community centers, and schools. Across the country, charitable bingo games have suffered striking revenue declines, a result, observers say, of an aging playing population but more significantly, the draw of other gambling outlets.

"Bingo is being cannibalized by the larger, faster games," said John Kindt, a professor of business and legal policy at the University of Illinois who studies legalized gambling.

A database compiled by Christiansen Capital Advisors, a Washington, D.C., consulting firm that advises the gaming industry, showed that overall consumer spending on bingo nationally has not changed since 1982, but charitable game revenue has fallen from an estimated $1.13 billion in 1998 to $974 million in 2001. The trend reflects what the firm's chairman, Eugene Christiansen, described as a "massive shift out of charitable games and into Indian games."

Here in Massachusetts, the number of licensed bingo games has declined by nearly half, going from 916 in 1984 to 479 in 2001. Meanwhile, annual attendance has plummeted from 10.4 million in 1984 to 3.7 million in 2001.

Bingo at Foxwoods, though, isn't lacking for players. Although Foxwoods opened the Connecticut casino in 1992, it has been running bingo games since 1986. Cedric Woods, a spokesman for the Mashantucket Pequot Tribe, which owns and operates Foxwoods, declined to make public its daily or annual bingo attendance numbers. But he characterized attendance as steady and said the casino's 3,500-person capacity bingo hall fills on special game days.

State lottery sales in Massachusetts also recently logged record highs, reaching $4.2 billion in fiscal year 2002, an increase of 6.8 percent over the previous year.

Local bingo operators say they can't compete with the burgeoning gambling options, when their payouts are so much smaller.

"Attendance has declined by at least 10 percent in the last couple of years," said Father Joseph Lahoud of Our Lady of the Cedars Church in Jamaica Plain [Boston neighborhood], where weekly game attendance now averages about 150. "We haven't had 200 in a long time. They tell me the people are going to Foxwoods. And you know, it's very sad. If we decline any further, no one will be interested in keeping the game going."

Loss of Community

The struggle—and death—of bingo games has meant less money in church choir coffers and fewer instruments for school bands, the traditional beneficiaries of charitable bingo, which was legalized in Massachusetts in 1971.

But some say the price must also be measured by another factor: loss of community cohesion.

"Bingo halls are rooted in geographic communities and reinforce social networks," said Thomas Sander, executive director of the Saguaro Seminar at Harvard University's Kennedy School of Government, which studies civic involvement. "If bingo players are going to Foxwoods, they are less likely to meet their neighbors."

Bingo is following in the path of other civic groups, Sander said, much like the Boy Scouts, PTAs, and Elks clubs, all of which have seen membership drop in recent years—a trend attributed to suburban sprawl, television, the aging of the World War II generation, and the increased number of working women with less time to devote to community activities.

One bright spot in the local bingo realm has been a change of state law two years ago, doubling the maximum prize for regular games from $50 to $100. It also broadened the pool of eligible volunteers.

State officials say the change has stanched the attendance decline. Weekly bingo attendance increased slightly between 2000 and 2001, from 69,805 to 70,402. But the number of games continued to drop, going from 504 in 2000 to 479 in 2001.

The figures suggest that small bingo games have continued to die, with players ending up at bigger games, sometimes one town over. Such is the case in Dennis on Cape Cod. The closure of a game in nearby Hyannis has meant a surge in attendance for the Dennis–Yarmouth Band Parents Bingo. On a recent Sunday evening, every chair was taken at the Dennis Senior Center, where the largely gray-haired crowd snacked on crumb cakes as the three-hour game got underway.

Val Perry, 30, a Yarmouth medical secretary, was hooked by her grandmother and now rarely misses Sunday games, where she puts down $40 and generally walks away with $75.

Foxwoods, where the ante to play a game is more, holds little allure. "If I went down there, I would spend tons," she said.

But tell that to Connie Tarantino, a diehard bingo fan who has played at the Nazzaro Center in the North End for years and now also travels to Connecticut. "At Foxwoods, the games are big—$300 and $500," she said.

"Yeah," said Helen Carbone, a fellow longtime bingo player. "But I can't hear a word they say."

Laughter rippled across the room, but only for a moment because the time had come. The women crossed themselves and prayed, focused heads downward, and waited for their moment of bingo glory.

Gambling on the Internet

Robin Gareiss and John Soat

As brick-and-mortar casinos reach a market satura-
tion point in the United States, many observers forecast that the next wave of growth for the gambling
industry will be on the Internet, where gamblers can
try their luck at casino-style games from the comfort
of home. In the following selection, Robin Gareiss
and John Soat examine the growth and appeal of this
burgeoning new outlet for gamblers. According to
the authors, the legality of online gambling for U.S.
residents currently falls in a gray area and may soon
be formally outlawed by congressional legislation.
Legal questions notwithstanding, large U.S. casino
operators are forging ahead with plans to run online
casinos from offshore locations. Enforcing a ban
against the thousands of U.S. residents who have already demonstrated a fondness for online gambling
may prove next to impossible, as Gareiss and Soat il-
lustrate. The authors are reporters for *Information-
Week*, a weekly technology magazine.

ODDS ARE, THE WINDY CITY OFFERS SOMETHING
for everyone—diverse architecture, a beautiful lakefront,
dozens of museums, and world-class restaurants. But 27-year-
old Scott Mauer hedged his bets with a different Chicago-area
attraction: the bevy of gambling outlets on riverboats, at racetracks, and even the state lottery. So when a job transfer led
him and his family to casino-free Tennessee two years ago, the

■

recreational gambler was concerned that he'd lose out on one of his favorite hobbies.

Gambling from the Comfort of Home

What he found instead was a jackpot—gambling over the Web. OK, so he doesn't hear the cheers of winners, the ringing of slot machines, or the crescendo of a track announcer. Complimentary drinks and showgirls are out of the picture, too. He's exchanged all that for convenience, ready access to information, and even a sense of security. "Online is 10 times easier than on-site," says Mauer, who frequents www.wsex.com, a sports-betting site run by World Sports Exchange Ltd., based and licensed in Antigua and Barbuda. "Compared to gambling with a bookie, you know you're going to get paid from sites that have been around. They'll put the money right in your account. You can do it in the comfort of your own home, and you have all the information you need on your computer."

Apparently, many others are buying into that appeal. The 200 companies that run about 2,000 online-gambling sites took in $2.5 billion in revenue last year, according to Informa-Media Group, which tracks electronic gambling. InformaMedia predicts that figure, still only 1% of conventional gambling revenue, will reach $14.5 billion by 2006. "Online gambling is one of the hottest sectors on the Internet," says Charles Buckwalter, an ad-tracking analyst formerly with Jupiter Media Metrix. The online-gambling industry got its start in 1998, driven by client-server technology, targeted marketing, the Web's global reach, and the human appetite for rolling the dice anytime, anywhere. It's a perfect business model for the Web. But as the market grows, online gambling is plagued by questions—not the least of which is whether it's even legal in the United States—and by problems such as banks' and credit card companies' refusal to accept transactions from gambling sites. Yet online-gambling operators and vendors of the technologies that power the sites continue to develop new games and venues, marketing programs, and payment options for their customers.

Gambling sites draw about 4.5 million people. These virtual casinos offer everything from blackjack to slot machines to sports betting to bingo. Typically, customers visit the sites, register, and deposit money via credit cards, checks, or person-to-person payment services such as PayPal and NETeller. Then they play their games of choice. When they win and want to cash out, they get their money in whatever form they choose.

For now, casino-style games and sports betting account for about 80% of online gambling's revenue, says Jean Noelting, president and CEO [chief executive officer] of CryptoLogic Inc., an online-gambling software and services provider. "We expect growth in the future from lottery, bingo, and poker," Noelting says. U.S. players represent about two-thirds of the revenue in online gambling. But the industry is looking to expand geographically, to maintain growth and to minimize the risk from legal hassles in the United States. "Europe and Asia are very underdeveloped," Noelting says.

The technology used in online gambling is basic clients-server architecture. Because startup costs are relatively low—a cheap server and some unsophisticated interactive software on the client side, which can be licensed from many sources—online-gambling sites pop up, and disappear, with regularity. Also, because of its rapid growth, online gambling seems to have replaced adult-oriented content as the platform of choice for the would-be Web entrepreneur. For those bent on breaking into the business, Yorktown Ventures Inc. in New York operates www.startcasino.com, a site that explains how to open an online casino. . . .

The Legal Issues

Virtually all the servers that run gambling sites are located outside the United States. CryptoLogic has server hubs in Argentina, the Caribbean, and the Isle of Man. That's because, according to federal and state laws, most online gambling is illegal in the United States.

Each of the four forms of legal gambling—horse racing, sports betting, casinos, and lotteries—has its own set of regulations. Horse-racing statutes are the most liberal. Federal law states that it's legal to take interstate horse-race wagers if it's legal in the sending and receiving states, says Anthony Cabot, a partner with Lionel Sawer, a Las Vegas law firm. Dozens of companies take wagers over the Internet and phone from several states.

Sports betting is the most conservative. The only state with legalized sports wagering is Nevada. Several Web sites, mostly startups with servers located in Central America and the Caribbean, take sports bets because they're outside of the United States' jurisdiction. They use foreign banks to transfer money, making it difficult for U.S. authorities to trace who's placing bets. Technically, it's illegal under U.S. law for the off-shore sites to take bets from U.S. residents living anywhere ex-

A First-Person Look at Online Gambling

I'll be dead by Tuesday.

That's what I thought when I was told to investigate how online gambling works. The only reason I don't spend every weekend at Nevada casinos is because they're in Nevada. Otherwise, I love it. The way the cards feel in my hand; the way the free drinks taste sliding down my throat; the way a 20 dollar bill looks shooting down the little slot in the blackjack table just before the dealer deals me my debt. But online casinos can't duplicate those feelings, right? I was supposed to find out.

Lose your money to the best, I always say. Based on InternetCasinoRankings.com's ranking criteria—software quality, customer service, fairness policies—Captain Cook's Casino is the best. I jumped right to the site and clicked on the "DOWNLOAD NOW" icon. I installed the software in just over a minute and was ready to go.

The Captain, like most online casinos, allows you to play for fun before playing for real money. Give him some basic info and you quickly get a feel for how to blow your savings. Although upgrades let you play 24 different games, only five are available with the basic download. I went straight for the blackjack table.

Ten minutes into the demo version, I'm relieved. Down $40, I hate online gambling. It's rigged, I've decided, and there's no way I could get sucked in to The

cept in Nevada, but they do. So far, federal law-enforcement agencies haven't pursued individual U.S. residents who bet on offshore sports sites. A few states, including New York and Minnesota, have threatened to do so, Cabot says.

Casinos and lotteries fall into a gray area. The statute most cited as governing lotteries and electronic casinos is the 1961 Federal Interstate Wireline Act. In essence, this law says that any bookie who uses wire communication between states or

Captain's wicked games. Twenty minutes later, I'm not so sure. After increasing my standard bet to $200, I'm up 1,700 demo dollars. Feeling lucky, I click on the large "REGISTER AS REAL USER" button, throw them my credit card number (which I know by heart, unfortunately) and immediately have a limit of $500 not-so-demo dollars.

I'm normally pretty skeptical when pretending to gamble in casinos named after famous explorers, so I was convinced the demo mode's odds were better than the real odds. I called to check, but The Captain's customer service team, which is docked somewhere in the United Kingdom (they can't say exactly where for security reasons) didn't have many answers. They said to email headquarters, but they never emailed me back. Thank God. Their answer was likely to be the same as most of the 1400 offshore casinos: they use a random number generator to create true odds, in demo and real play mode. I would have convinced myself to play for real dough, and undoubtedly would have lost it all. I didn't, sticking to demo mode and eventually closing my real account.

Logic—and my mom, probably—say I should have deleted the software immediately. I didn't, but I will soon, when I get around to it.

Just a couple more hands.

Anonymous testimony submitted to the House Committee on Financial Services Hearing, "Financial Aspects of Internet Gaming: Good Gamble or Bad Bet?" July 12, 2001.

between a state and a foreign country to take bets on any sporting event or contest is guilty of a felony. The confusion relates to the words "sporting event or contest." The Justice Department says "sporting" modifies "event," and the word "contest" covers everything else. Online gambling advocates say the word "sporting" modifies "event" and "contest," and therefore applies only to sports betting, Cabot says. What's more, some question whether the Internet is covered under "wire communication" because the law referred to phone wires when it was written.

State laws, many of which prohibit gambling beyond state-sponsored lotteries, don't appear to be in online gambling's favor. "Accepting casino-style wagering is probably illegal under most state laws," Cabot says. "But most state laws were adopted 200 years ago, so the question is, how do they apply to the Internet?"

Looming Regulation

Two things could clear up the uncertainty. The first is federal legislation to deal specifically with online gambling. The House of Representatives Subcommittee on Crime is examining legislation proposed by Representative Bob Goodlatte, R-Va., that would make all forms of Internet betting illegal in the United States.

The second is a pending ruling by the 5th U.S. Circuit Court of Appeals, stemming from a class-action case that went before the New Orleans federal court two years ago [2000]. In the suit, attorneys argued that credit-card companies damaged their clients, who were online gamblers, by allowing them to use credit cards on gambling sites. They said it was a violation of the Federal Interstate Wireline Act, but the court ruled that the law doesn't apply to online casino gambling, just to sports betting. The appellate court is expected to rule this year on whether the act applies.

In the meantime, Mauer will continue gambling online. "The legal issues concern me, but then they really don't," he says. "I'm not afraid of the IRS going after me. With the amount of money I wager, I don't worry about it." But he advocates legislation that protects the consumer. "I'd like to see some kind of legislation that prevents Joe Schmo from opening a sports book for a few weeks, then closing and ripping people off. It's happening all the time."

Even if the U.S. government starts regulating Internet gambling, many players will continue to prefer offshore sites so that they can use foreign banks to avoid claiming their winnings on their tax returns, says Ron Carter, chairman of the Internet Gaming Commission, an industry-advocacy group. "People have money that they don't want the government to know they have," he says. "None of that information will ever be transmitted to the government" by offshore operators. If the government explicitly allows online gambling, it could mandate that the online casinos report who wagered more than, say, $10,000 in the past month. "That could be part of the rules to make this legal within the U.S."

Legal questions aren't the only problems that confront online gambling. Banks that issue credit cards present a huge challenge for the sites and their customers. Most recently, Citibank, which controls about 12% of U.S. credit-card business, said it would no longer accept transactions from online-gambling sites, joining a group that includes Bank of America, Chase Manhattan, Direct Merchants, Fleet, and MBNA. Credit-card issuers that do accept those transactions typically hold half or all of the money for six months to one year to make sure consumers don't dispute the charges and indeed pay their bills, Carter says. Since banks began rejecting the transactions, the online-gambling industry has lost $500 million to $1 billion in revenue, he adds. "A substantial portion of online transactions are done with credit cards," Las Vegas lawyer Cabot says. But setbacks like that are usually temporary, he says. "Once you throw out an obstacle, someone will find a way around it.". . .

Person-to-person payment sites, such as PayPal and NETeller, are emerging as an alternative to credit cards for online-gambling transactions. They transfer money directly into and out of customers' bank or credit-card accounts. For the online-gambling operators, though, this option doesn't come cheap: PayPal, for instance, charges the casinos an average of 8.5% per transaction, Carter says. Some payment sites, by masking gambling debts, may even allow online gamblers to skirt the credit-card ban. Not PayPal, says a spokesman.

The company codes gaming transactions so that credit-card issuers recognize them.

As online-gambling revenue climbs, conventional casinos must walk a fine line. They want to be involved in a growing market, yet they don't want to risk breaking laws by encouraging their U.S. customers to gamble online. MGM Mirage, Station Association, and Sun International are the land-based gaming companies with the most aggressive online-gambling strategies, says Marc Falcone, former leisure and gaming analyst with Bear Steams, now with DeutscheBank. MGM Mirage runs its Internet operation from the Isle of Man, a British territory, to offer online gambling in Europe and other parts of the world where it's legal. "The larger companies are going to jump in, at least on an offshore-to-offshore basis," Cabot says. "It's not a question of if, but how."

For MGM Mirage, at least, the "how" has to do with the software it's using from WagerWorks. Andrew Pascal [president and CEO of WagerWorks, Inc.] says his company has spent considerable time developing technology that's "regulatory-based," that can verify where a potential customer is from and how old that potential customer is. "We focused on regulatory issues," Pascal says. "We understand them. We know how to deal with them."

Most major U.S. casinos want to leverage the Web just as the traditional click-and-mortar pioneers did. And there are ways to deal with the law. Some U.S. casinos offer play-for-free games online. Customers can earn tokens or certificates that they can redeem for prizes or use when they go to the brick-and-mortar casinos. "They'll give you two nights for free or send you a T-shirt," Carter says. "They're just building a following." Most industry observers pooh-pooh the idea that online gambling will cannibalize the land-based casinos. "We think it's going to help expand that marketplace," Falcone says. "There are cross-marketing opportunities meant to drive physical visitations to the casinos."

The biggest challenge for online gambling these days is customer acquisition and retention. That's why the more sophisticated online-gambling sites use personalization and customer-support software, in much the same way booksellers or airlines do. They create profiles of their customers, track their activities, and offer promotions to lure them back to the sites. Online casinos have an edge over their bricks-and-mortar counterparts in most cases, because it's easier to track who's doing what online than it is in a physical casino. Online, each gambler must register and use a log-on each time he or she visits a site. "They do know a lot more about you online," Carter says.

One way gambling sites have expanded their potential customer base is by buying pop-up-ad space from search engines and portals, a shift in their approach to advertising on the Web that's serving them well, says analyst Buckwalter. Last year, most of the advertising for online-gambling sites was placed on niche gaming sites. This year, about half of the industry's 2.5-billion-plus ads are showing up on mainstream portals to attract new customers who may not even know online-gambling sites exist. "The wide reach and impact is serving them very well," Buckwalter says. "Online gambling's reputation has been on the underbelly of the Internet. This change in strategy has helped."

Image, Fraud Problems Abound

Maybe. The online-gambling industry has its problems. It grew very quickly, creating Web sites that went out of business before gamblers could recoup their money. That's given the online-gambling industry an image problem. "A lot of these sites are scams," Mauer says. "They'll open for two weeks, take your money, and then shut down." The industry is littered with scams, on both sides. The casinos don't always deliver what they promise, and some consumers have found ways around glitches in the gaming software that runs the sites so they can win money unfairly. Customer-acquisition costs have risen because companies haven't figured out who their best prospects are and how to effectively market to them, Falcone says. What's more, lawmakers are concerned that the sites offer organized-crime groups a simple way to launder money.

The online-gambling community has attempted its own damage control. For instance, Majorwager.com, an online gambling site that runs pop-up ads for casinos, provides a listing of sites that it recommends people avoid.

The Internet Gaming Commission, formed about 2½ years ago [2000], provides a portal to gaming sites and resolution of consumer complaints. The commission doesn't test the sites. Instead, it relies on consumers' reporting whether they've had bad experiences, and it keeps a database of each gaming site. It provides links only to sites that have high ratings among customers. "We write to the gaming sites and tell them of allegations," Carter says. "Most of the time, we get a very good response."

Because gamblers register with the sites, gaming software can track how successful they were during their visits. Consumers often complain that they didn't win enough money or that a site was rigged. "But the sites can come back and say, 'This person has a 98.35% win rate,'" because of the software, Carter says. (A win rate reflects how much the game has paid out to an individual but doesn't factor in how much of those winnings he or she continues to wager—and often loses.)

For the most part, Carter says, casinos don't have to cheat because the odds are in their favor. But some are undercapitalized, which gives them an incentive to delay payments. A gamer could win $2,000, and a site promises to send his money within 24 hours: "They'll stall and give you excuses. Then you get frustrated and gamble it all away."

Online casinos face their own problems with fraud. For example, some gamblers use stolen credit cards to start their accounts. When they win, many sites will credit only $500 back to their credit cards and mail the rest. Now, the casinos mandate that customers fax them copies of their driver's licenses to verify their addresses and identities.

And like any other Internet citizens, online-gambling sites have problems with hackers. Last year, hackers broke into CryptoLogic servers and "caused higher win rates in certain games," according to the company. In the end, gamblers won $1.9 million before CryptoLogic discovered the attack.

Moving forward, industry observers expect that innovation will drive online gambling into new areas. "There's a big business opportunity," Cabot says. He expects a convergence of gaming, such as video games or other online games, and gambling. When people play skill games online, they could bet on who will win. So rather than having one person play blackjack against the computer, sites will start offering multiplayer options.

No matter how the laws shape up, the technology will work its way around them. There's online-casino software that blocks out IP [Internet provider] addresses based in the United States and Canada, so even if law-enforcement agencies wanted to prosecute online gamblers, they would have a tough time tracking them down because there's no record of the site visits. While other dot-com industries have crashed and burned, online gambling has taken off. Despite the potential for some serious setbacks, smart money says it's a good bet to keep growing.

FOR FURTHER RESEARCH

Herbert Asbury, *Sucker's Progress: An Informal History of Gambling in America from the Colonies to Canfield.* New York: Dodd, Mead, 1938.
> In this overview of America's history of gambling, Asbury describes how professional gamblers traveled far and wide, spreading the gospel of gambling to cities and towns from coast to coast. As the title implies, the book is written in an informal, often humorous style.

Andy Bellin, *Poker Nation: A High-Stakes, Low-Life Adventure into the Heart of a Gambling Country.* New York: HarperCollins, 2002.
> Bellin, an avid poker player, examines how America's favorite card game has instilled itself into popular culture. He offers advice on playing the game and recounts the exploits of poker fanatics in card clubs, both legal and illegal, across the country.

Jeff Benedict, *Without Reservation: The Making of America's Most Powerful Indian Tribe and Foxwoods, the World's Largest Casino.* New York: HarperCollins, 2000.
> Benedict chronicles the rise of the Mashantucket Pequot tribe, which opened the phenomenally successful Foxwoods casino in rural Connecticut in 1992. The tribe would come to wield enormous political influence and economic power, antagonizing businesspeople and the local community along the way.

Jeff Burbank, *License to Steal: Nevada's Gaming Control System in the Megaresort Age.* Reno: University of Nevada Press, 2000.
> This book traces the history of legalized gambling in Nevada, from its origins and connection to organized crime figures to the state's efforts to clean up the gambling industry through stricter regulation and licensing requirements.

Charles T. Clotfelter and Philip J. Cook, *Selling Hope: State Lotteries in America.* Cambridge, MA: Harvard University Press, 1989.
> This book provides a historical overview of lotteries in American culture. Periods of prohibition notwithstanding, the authors demonstrate how lotteries have remained consistently popular with urban Americans.

Richard O. Davies and Richard G. Abram, *Betting the Line: Sports Wagering in American Life*. Columbus: Ohio State University Press, 2001.

The authors provide a detailed analysis of how widespread betting on college and professional sports is directly responsible for the enormous popularity of sports in American life. Americans wager billions of dollars each year in office betting pools, with illegal bookies, and with Nevada sports books, relishing the added excitement betting brings to sporting events.

Robert K. DeArment, *Knights of the Green Cloth: The Saga of the Frontier Gamblers*. Norman: University of Oklahoma Press, 1982.

Following the opening of the Louisiana Purchase to U.S. settlement in 1803, gambling experienced enormous popularity as it spread from New Orleans to towns across the western frontier. DeArment presents a thorough history of gambling's unique role in the settlement of the United States.

Jeffrey W. Dement, *Going for Broke: The Depiction of Compulsive Gambling in Film*. Lanham, MD: Scarecrow, 1999.

The spread of legalized gambling has led to increasing numbers of Americans with uncontrollable gambling habits, known as compulsive gambling. In this book, Dement examines how compulsive gambling is portrayed in several popular films, including *Fever Pitch*, *The Gambler*, and *Vegas Vacation*. The author contends that, with few exceptions, Hollywood filmmakers portray both compulsive gamblers and gambling in an irresponsible manner.

Sally Denton and Roger Morris, *The Money and the Power: The Making of Las Vegas and Its Hold on America, 1947–2000*. New York: Knopf, 2001.

Denton and Morris chronicle the seedy roots of legalized gambling in Las Vegas from the days of gangsters in the 1940s to the billion-dollar casino resorts of the 1990s. The authors contend that the city's rise to cultural preeminence at the turn of the century is a reflection of the greed and corruption endemic in American social and political life.

John Samuel Ezell, *Fortune's Merry Wheel: The Lottery in America*. Cambridge, MA: Harvard University Press, 1960.

Ezell traces the history of the lottery in American culture from the colonial era to the years following World War II. The author examines how lotteries, once a widespread and popular form of entertainment, fell victim to a backlash in the late 1800s after scandals involving theft and fraud were exposed to the public. The book was published a few years before New Hampshire reintroduced a state lottery in 1963 and launched a lottery boom that rapidly spread to several other states.

John M. Findlay, *People of Chance: Gambling in American Society from Jamestown to Las Vegas.* New York: Oxford University Press, 1986.

Beginning with the colonial era, Findlay describes how gambling emerged as a popular expression of the risk, chance, and search for instant wealth that characterized the settlement of America. The book includes an analysis of Las Vegas's transformation from a dusty railroad town to the rollicking Strip of the post–World War II era.

Robert Goodman, *The Luck Business: The Devastating Consequences and Broken Promises of America's Gambling Explosion.* New York: Free Press, 1995.

Goodman explores the downside of America's new gambling economy, including dependency of governments on gambling revenues, the proliferation of Indian casinos, and the troubling legacy of convenience gambling.

Nelson Johnson, *Boardwalk Empire: The Birth, High Times, and Corruption of Atlantic City.* Medford, NJ: Plexus, 2002.

In 1978, the state of New Jersey legalized casino gambling along the boardwalk in Atlantic City, a seaside resort that had fallen on hard times. Johnson examines Atlantic City's transformation from a quiet town into the Atlantic coast's center of casino gambling. He also reveals the corruption and political racketeering that went on behind the scenes.

Jackson Lears, *Something for Nothing: Luck in America.* New York: Viking, 2003.

Lears examines the conflict between America's Protestant work ethic and the public's growing tolerance for legalized gambling. The author contends that reverence for luck, chance, and gambling have had a formidable, yet often overlooked, impact on the national character.

Andres Martinez, *24/7: Living It Up and Doubling Down in the New Las Vegas.* New York: Dell Books, 2000.

Armed with fifty thousand dollars and an Ivy League education, the author arrives in Las Vegas and immerses himself in the city's fantastical culture of twenty-four-hour gambling. The book offers observations on the massive theme resorts built to attract families during the 1990s and true-life tales of family men who lost it all under the spell of the casinos.

Barry Meadow, *Blackjack Autumn: A True Tale of Life, Death, and Splitting Tens in Winnemucca.* Anaheim, CA: TR Publishing, 1999.

In this overview of casino gambling in Nevada, the author hits the road with ten thousand dollars in his pocket, intending to play blackjack in every casino in the state. The book offers unique observations on Nevada's casino gambling culture from the perspective of a professional card player.

Ben Mezrich, *Bringing Down the House: The Inside Story of Six MIT Students Who Took Vegas for Millions.* New York: Free Press, 2002.

This book relates the true tale of six students from the Massachusetts Institute of Technology who started a blackjack club while in college and learned the techniques of "card counting" to beat the odds. The students took their gambit to Las Vegas, where they won millions before being discovered by casino authorities.

Angela Mullis and David Kemper, eds., *Indian Gaming: Who Wins?* Los Angeles: University of California, American Indian Studies Center, 2001.

This anthology covers the numerous social and political issues that have arisen in American culture following the Indian Gaming and Regulatory Act of 1988, which set the terms under which Indian tribes could run casinos on tribal lands. Topics covered include growing white resentment of Indian casinos and the impact of casinos on tribal culture.

David Nibert, *Hitting the Lottery Jackpot: Government and the Taxing of Dreams.* New York: Monthly Review Press/New York University Press, 1999.

The author contends that government-run lotteries prey on the dreams of poor Americans, who regularly spend their money on tickets but stand little chance of winning. Governments have become too dependent on the revenues generated by lotteries, which, in the author's opinion, are regressive taxes on the poor.

Timothy L. O'Brien, *Bad Bet: The Inside Story of the Glamour, Glitz, and Danger of America's Gambling Industry.* New York: Random House, 1998.

The political and social forces behind legalized gambling's massive expansion over the past twenty-five years are the subject of this book. The author concedes that, although gambling is rife with troubling consequences, America's love for gambling is irrepressible; he also indicates that legalized gambling may be here to stay.

Hunter S. Thompson, *Fear and Loathing in Las Vegas and Other American Stories.* New York: Modern Library, 1998.

Journalist Thompson recounts, in vivid detail, a drug-induced odyssey to Las Vegas in 1971. The book offers a timeless description of Las Vegas, which the author contends is an apt metaphor for the failure of the American Dream.

Mike Tronnes, ed., *Literary Las Vegas: The Best Writing About America's Most Fabulous City.* New York: Henry Holt, 1995.

In this anthology of essays describing the popular appeal of Las Vegas, writers like Joan Didion, Hunter S. Thompson, and Noel Coward offer their thoughts and impressions on America's gambling capital.

Mike Weatherford, *Cult Vegas: The Weirdest! The Wildest! The Swingin'est Town on Earth!* Las Vegas: Huntington Press, 2001.

Weatherford presents an overview of Las Vegas casino culture and its influence on American popular culture. The gambling capital has inspired Frank Sinatra and his Rat Pack pals, the wild flamboyance of Elvis Presley, schmaltzy "lounge" culture, showgirls, and countless Hollywood movies with a Las Vegas theme.

INDEX